United States Government Accountability Office

By the Comptroller General of the United States

# GAO

July 2007

# Government Auditing Standards

## July 2007 Revision

D1376653

The July 2007 revision of Government Auditing Standards supersedes the 2003 revision and updates the January 2007 revision. The July 2007 revision represents the complete 2007 revision of Government Auditing Standards, and is the version that should be used by government auditors until further updates and revisions are made. An electronic version of this document can be accessed on GAO's Yellow Book Web page at http://www.gao.gov/govaud/ybk01.htm.

The July 2007 revision of Government Auditing Standards will be effective for financial audits and attestation engagements for periods beginning on or after January 1, 2008, and for performance audits beginning on or after January 1, 2008. Early implementation is permissible and encouraged. For financial audits, certain standards of the Auditing Standards Board (ASB) that affect Government Auditing Standards become effective prior to these dates.

For sale by the Superintendent of Documents, U.S. Government Printing Office
Internet: bookstore.gpo.gov   Phone: toll free (866) 512-1800;   DC area (202) 512-1800
Fax: (202) 512-2104 Mail: Stop IDCC, Washington, DC 20402-0001

ISBN 978-0-16-078028-8

# Contents

## Abbreviations

| | |
|---|---|
| AICPA | American Institute of Certified Public Accountants |
| AU | AICPA *Codification of Statements on Auditing Standards* |
| CPA | certified public accountant |
| CPE | continuing professional education |
| COSO | Committee of Sponsoring Organizations of the Treadway Commission |
| GAAP | generally accepted accounting principles |
| GAGAS | generally accepted government auditing standards |
| GAO | U.S. Government Accountability Office |
| IAASB | International Auditing and Assurance Standards Board |
| IIA | Institute of Internal Auditors |
| ISA | International Statements on Auditing |
| ISACA | Information Systems Audit and Control Association |
| MD&A | management's discussion and analysis |
| OMB | U.S. Office of Management and Budget |
| PCAOB | Public Company Accounting Oversight Board |
| SAS | Statements on Auditing Standards |
| SSAE | Statements on Standards for Attestation Engagements |

The principles of transparency and accountability for the use of public resources are key to our nation's governing processes. Government officials and recipients of federal moneys are responsible for carrying out public functions efficiently, economically, effectively, ethically, and equitably, while achieving desired program objectives. High-quality auditing is essential for government accountability to the public and transparency regarding linking resources to related program results. Auditing of government programs should provide independent, objective, fact-based, nonpartisan assessments of the stewardship, performance, and cost of government policies, programs, and operations. Government audits also provide key information to stakeholders and the public to maintain accountability; help improve program performance and operations; reduce costs; facilitate decision making; stimulate improvements; and identify current and projected crosscutting issues and trends that affect government programs and the people those programs serve.

The professional standards presented in this document provide a framework for performing high-quality audit work with competence, integrity, objectivity, and independence. I firmly believe that government auditors should lead by example in the areas of transparency, performance, accountability, and quality through the audit process.

Current trends and longer-range fiscal challenges make auditor oversight especially important to help improve government operations and services today and position them for a better tomorrow. Government auditing plays a major role in improving government operations and services, and in the important dialogue on the future of government programs by providing the objective analysis and information needed to make the decisions necessary to help create a better future. GAO will continue its efforts to lead by example in all of these areas.

The July 2007 revision of *Government Auditing Standards* supersedes the 2003 revision and updates the January 2007 revision. This revision contains the January 2007 revision plus updated quality control and peer review sections in chapter 3 which were exposed in January 2007. The July 2007 revision represents the completed 2007 revision of *Government Auditing Standards*, and is the version that should be used by government auditors until further updates and revisions are made. An electronic version of this document can be accessed on the Web at http://www.gao.gov/govaud/ybk01.htm.

This revision contains the following fundamental changes from the 2003 revision that reinforce the principles of transparency and accountability and provide the framework for high-quality government audits that add value.

- Heightened the emphasis on ethical principles as the foundation, discipline, and structure behind the implementation of the standards, including a description of five key ethical principles that should guide the work of those who audit government programs and operations.

- Clarified and streamlined the discussion of the impact of professional services other than audits or attestation engagements (nonaudit services) and their impact on auditor independence.

- Enhanced and clarified the requirements for an audit organization's system of quality control by specifying the elements of quality that an organization's policies and procedures should collectively address.

- Added a requirement that external audit organizations make their most recent peer review reports publicly available.

- Updated the financial auditing standards based on recent developments in financial auditing and internal control, increased transparency surrounding restatements, and significant concerns, uncertainties, or other unusual events that could have a significant impact on the financial condition or operations of a government entity or program.

- Enhanced performance auditing standards that elaborate on the overall framework for high-quality performance auditing, including the concepts of reasonable assurance and its relationship to audit risk, significance, and the levels of evidence used to support audit findings and conclusions.

- Clarified the standards through standardized language to define the auditor's level of responsibility and distinguish between auditor requirements and additional guidance.

- Reinforced the key role of auditing in maintaining accountability and providing information for making improvements in government operations.

This revision of the standards has gone through an extensive deliberative process, including public comments and input from the Comptroller General's Advisory Council on Government Auditing Standards. The Advisory Council generally consists of about 25 experts in financial and performance auditing and reporting drawn from federal, state, and local government; the private sector; and academia. The views of all parties were thoroughly considered in finalizing the standards.

The July 2007 revision of *Government Auditing Standards* will be effective for financial audits and attestation engagements for periods beginning on or after January 1, 2008, and for performance audits beginning on or after January 1, 2008. Early implementation is permissible and encouraged. For financial audits, certain standards of the Auditing Standards Board (ASB) that affect *Government Auditing Standards* become effective prior to these dates. We encourage audit organizations to implement the relevant sections of the 2007 revision for financial audits concurrent with the implementation of the related ASB standards.

I extend special thanks to the members of the Advisory Council for their extensive input and feedback through the entire process of developing and finalizing the standards.

David M. Walker
Comptroller General
of the United States

July 2007

# Chapter 1

# Use and Application of GAGAS

## Introduction

**1.01** Auditing is essential to government accountability to the public. Audits and attestation engagements provide an independent, objective, nonpartisan assessment of the stewardship, performance, or cost of government policies, programs, or operations, depending upon the type and scope of the audit.

**1.02** The concept of accountability for use of public resources and government authority is key to our nation's governing processes. Government officials entrusted with public resources are responsible for carrying out public functions legally, effectively, efficiently, economically, ethically, and equitably.[1] Government managers are responsible for providing reliable, useful, and timely information for accountability of government programs and their operations. (See appendix I paragraph A1.08 for additional information on management's responsibility.) Legislators, government officials, and the public need to know whether (1) government manages public resources and uses its authority properly and in compliance with laws and regulations; (2) government programs are achieving their objectives and desired outcomes; (3) government services are provided effectively, efficiently, economically, ethically, and equitably; and (4) government managers are held accountable for their use of public resources.

## Purpose and Applicability of GAGAS

**1.03** The professional standards and guidance contained in this document, commonly referred to as generally accepted government auditing standards (GAGAS), provide a framework for conducting high quality

---

[1] The term "equity" in this context refers to the approaches used by a government, nonprofit, or other organizations that manage or carry out government programs to provide services to the public in a fair manner within the context of the statutory boundaries of the specific government programs.

government audits and attestation engagements with competence, integrity, objectivity, and independence. These standards are for use by auditors[2] of government entities and entities that receive government awards and audit organizations[3] performing GAGAS audits and attestation engagements. GAGAS contain requirements and guidance dealing with ethics, independence, auditors' professional competence and judgment, quality control, the performance of field work, and reporting. Audits and attestation engagements performed under GAGAS provide information used for oversight, accountability, and improvements of government programs and operations. GAGAS contain requirements and guidance to assist auditors in objectively acquiring and evaluating sufficient, appropriate evidence and reporting the results. When auditors perform their work in this manner and comply with GAGAS in reporting the results, their work can lead to improved government management, better decision making and oversight, effective and efficient operations, and accountability for resources and results.

1.04 Laws, regulations, contracts, grant agreements, or policies frequently require audits in accordance with GAGAS. Many auditors and audit organizations also voluntarily choose to perform their work in accordance with GAGAS. The requirements and guidance in this document apply to audits and attestation engagements of government entities, programs, activities, and functions, and of government assistance administered by contractors, nonprofit entities, and other

---

[2]The term "auditor" throughout this document includes individuals performing work under GAGAS (including audits and attestation engagements) and, therefore, individuals who may have the titles auditor, analyst, evaluator, inspector, or other similar titles.

[3]The term "audit organization" is used throughout the standards to refer to government audit organizations as well as public accounting firms that perform audits using GAGAS.

nongovernmental entities when the use of GAGAS is required or is voluntarily followed.

## Use of Terminology to Define Professional Requirements in GAGAS

**1.05** GAGAS contain professional requirements together with related guidance in the form of explanatory material.[4] Auditors have a responsibility to consider the entire text of GAGAS in carrying out their work and in understanding and applying the professional requirements in GAGAS.

**1.06** Not every paragraph of GAGAS carries a professional requirement that auditors and audit organizations are expected to fulfill. Rather, the professional requirements are identified through use of specific language.

**1.07** GAGAS use two categories of professional requirements, identified by specific terms, to describe the degree of responsibility they impose on auditors and audit organizations, as follows:

a. Unconditional requirements: Auditors and audit organizations are required to comply with an unconditional requirement in all cases in which the circumstances exist to which the unconditional requirement applies. GAGAS use the words *must* or *is required* to specify an unconditional requirement.

b. Presumptively mandatory requirements: Auditors and audit organizations are also required to comply with a presumptively mandatory requirement in all cases in which the circumstances exist to which the

---

[4]The terminology used in GAGAS to designate professional requirements and explanatory material is intended to be consistent with the American Institute of Certified Public Accountants (AICPA) Statement on Auditing Standard No. 102, *Defining Professional Requirements in Statements on Auditing Standards.*

presumptively mandatory requirement applies; however, in rare circumstances, auditors and audit organizations may depart from a presumptively mandatory requirement provided they document their justification for the departure and how the alternative procedures performed in the circumstances were sufficient to achieve the objectives of the presumptively mandatory requirement. GAGAS use the word *should* to specify a presumptively mandatory requirement.

**1.08** Explanatory material is defined as the text within GAGAS (including appendix I) other than the requirements defined in paragraph 1.07. Explanatory material uses the words *may, might,* and *could* to describe explanatory information and is provided to

**a.** provide further explanation and guidance on the professional requirements or

**b.** identify and describe other procedures or actions relating to auditors' or audit organizations' activities.

**1.09** Explanatory material is intended to be descriptive rather than required. This material is intended, for example, to explain the objective of a requirement where it would be useful to do so; explain why particular procedures may be considered or employed under certain circumstances; or provide additional information to consider in exercising professional judgment.

**1.10** Explanatory material that identifies and describes other procedures or actions does not impose a professional requirement on the auditor or audit organization to perform the suggested procedures or actions. How and whether to carry out such procedures or actions depends on the exercise of professional judgment consistent with the objective of the standard.

**Stating Compliance with GAGAS in the Auditors' Report**

**1.11** When auditors are required to follow GAGAS or are representing to others that they followed GAGAS, they should follow all applicable GAGAS requirements and should refer to compliance with GAGAS in the auditors' report as set forth in paragraphs 1.12 and 1.13.

**1.12** Auditors should include one of the following types of GAGAS compliance statements in reports on GAGAS audits and attestation engagements, as appropriate.[5]

**a.** Unmodified GAGAS compliance statement: Stating that the auditor performed the audit or attestation engagement in accordance with GAGAS. Auditors should include an unmodified GAGAS compliance statement in the audit report when they have (1) followed all applicable unconditional and presumptively mandatory GAGAS requirements, or (2) have followed all unconditional requirements and documented justification for any departures from applicable presumptively mandatory requirements, and have achieved the objectives of those requirements through other means.

**b.** Modified GAGAS compliance statement: Stating either that (1) the auditor performed the audit or attestation engagement in accordance with GAGAS, except for specific applicable requirements that were not followed, or (2) because of the significance of the departure(s) from the requirements, the auditor was unable to and did not perform the audit or attestation engagement in accordance with GAGAS. Situations when auditors use modified compliance statements include scope limitations, such as restrictions on access to records, government officials, or other individuals

---

[5]For financial audits and attestation engagements, AICPA reporting standards provide additional guidance when some or all of the standards are not followed.

needed to conduct the audit. When auditors use a modified GAGAS statement, they should disclose in the report the applicable requirement(s) not followed, the reasons for not following the requirement(s), and how not following the requirements affected, or could have affected, the audit and the assurance provided.

**1.13** When auditors do not comply with any applicable requirements, they should (1) assess the significance of the noncompliance to the audit objectives, (2) document the assessment, along with their reasons for not following the requirement, and (3) determine the type of GAGAS compliance statement.[6] The auditors' determination will depend on the significance of the requirements not followed in relation to the audit objectives.

## Relationship between GAGAS and Other Professional Standards

**1.14** Auditors may use GAGAS in conjunction with professional standards issued by other authoritative bodies. Auditors may also cite the use of other standards in their audit reports, as appropriate. If the auditor is citing compliance with GAGAS and inconsistencies exist between GAGAS and other standards cited, the auditor should use GAGAS as the prevailing standard for conducting the audit and reporting the results.

**1.15** The relationship between GAGAS and other professional standards for financial audits and attestation engagements is as follows:

**a.** The American Institute of Certified Public Accountants (AICPA) has established professional standards that apply to financial audits and attestation

---

[6]See footnote 35 for applicability of peer review and quality assurance requirements in this assessment.

engagements for nonissuers[7] performed by certified public accountants (CPA). For financial audits, GAGAS incorporate the AICPA field work and reporting standards and the related Statements on Auditing Standards (SAS)[8] unless specifically excluded or modified by GAGAS. For attestation engagements, GAGAS incorporate the AICPA general standard on criteria, and the field work and reporting standards and the related Statements on Standards for Attestation Engagements (SSAE) unless specifically excluded or modified by GAGAS. GAGAS describe ethical principles, and establish independence and other general standards, and additional field work and reporting standards beyond those provided by the AICPA for performing financial audits and attestation engagements.

**b.** The Public Company Accounting Oversight Board (PCAOB) has established professional standards that apply to financial audits and attestation engagements for issuers. Auditors may use GAGAS in conjunction with the PCAOB standards.

**c.** The International Auditing and Assurance Standards Board (IAASB) has established professional standards that apply to financial audits and attestation engagements. Auditors may use GAGAS in conjunction

---

[7]Under the Sarbanes-Oxley Act of 2002 (Public Law 107-204), audits of issuers (generally, publicly traded companies with a reporting obligation under the Securities Exchange Act of 1934) are subject to rules and standards established by the Public Company Accounting Oversight Board. The term "nonissuer" refers to any entity other than an issuer under the Sarbanes-Oxley Act of 2002, such as privately held companies, nonprofit entities, and government entities.

[8]Because GAGAS incorporate the field work and reporting standards of the AICPA for financial audits performed in which U.S. auditing standards are to be followed, auditors are not required to cite compliance with the AICPA standards when citing compliance with GAGAS, although auditors may cite both sets of standards.

with the IAASB standards and the related statements on International Statements on Auditing (ISA).

**1.16** For performance audits, auditors may use other professional standards in conjunction with GAGAS, such as the following:

**a.** *International Standards for the Professional Practice of Internal Auditing*, The Institute of Internal Auditors, Inc.;

**b.** *Guiding Principles for Evaluators*, American Evaluation Association;

**c.** *The Program Evaluation Standards*, Joint Committee on Standards for Education Evaluation; and

**d.** *Standards for Educational and Psychological Testing*, American Psychological Association.

## Types of GAGAS Audits and Attestation Engagements

**1.17** This section describes the types of audits and attestation engagements that audit organizations may perform under GAGAS. This description is not intended to limit or require the types of audits or attestation engagements that may be performed under GAGAS.

**1.18** All audits and attestation engagements begin with objectives, and those objectives determine the type of audit to be performed and the applicable standards to be followed. The types of audits that are covered by GAGAS, as defined by their objectives, are classified in this document as financial audits, attestation engagements, and performance audits.

**1.19** In some audits and attestation engagements, the standards applicable to the specific audit objective will be apparent. For example, if the audit objective is to express an opinion on financial statements, the standards for financial audits apply. However, some engagements may have multiple or overlapping objectives. For example, if the objectives are to determine the reliability of performance measures, this work can be done in accordance with either the standards for attestation engagements or for performance audits. In cases in which there is a choice between applicable standards, auditors should evaluate users' needs and the auditors' knowledge, skills, and experience in deciding which standards to follow.

**1.20** GAGAS requirements apply to the types of audit and attestation engagements that may be performed under GAGAS as follows:

**a.** Financial audits: chapters 1 through 5 apply.

**b.** Attestation engagements: chapters 1 through 3 and 6 apply.

**c.** Performance audits: chapters 1 through 3 and 7 and 8 apply.

**1.21** Appendix I includes supplemental guidance for auditors and the audited entities to assist in the implementation of GAGAS. Appendix I does not establish auditor requirements but instead is intended to facilitate auditor implementation of the standards contained in chapters 1 through 8.

## Financial Audits

**1.22** Financial audits provide an independent assessment of and reasonable assurance about whether an entity's reported financial condition, results, and use of resources are presented fairly in accordance with recognized criteria. Reporting on financial audits performed in accordance with GAGAS also includes reports on internal control, compliance with laws and regulations, and provisions of contracts and grant agreements as they relate to financial transactions, systems, and processes. Financial audits performed under GAGAS include financial statement audits and other related financial audits:

**a. Financial statement audits:** The primary purpose of a financial statement audit is to provide reasonable assurance through an opinion (or disclaim an opinion) about whether an entity's financial statements are presented fairly in all material respects in conformity with generally accepted accounting principles (GAAP),[9] or with a comprehensive basis of accounting other than GAAP.

**b.** Other types of financial audits: Other types of financial audits under GAGAS provide for different levels of assurance and entail various scopes of work, including: (1) providing special reports, such as for specified elements, accounts, or items of a financial statement;[10] (2) reviewing interim financial information;[11] (3) issuing letters for underwriters and certain other requesting parties; (4) reporting on the controls over

---

[9]The three U.S.-based authoritative bodies for establishing accounting principles and financial reporting standards are the Federal Accounting Standards Advisory Board (federal government), the Governmental Accounting Standards Board (state and local governments), and the Financial Accounting Standards Board (nongovernmental entities).

[10]Special reports are auditors' reports issued in connection with the following: (1) financial statements that are prepared in conformity with a comprehensive basis of accounting other than generally accepted accounting principles; (2) specified elements, accounts, or items of a financial statement; (3) compliance with aspects of contractual agreements or regulatory requirements related to audited financial statements; (4) financial presentations to comply with contractual agreements or regulatory requirements; or (5) financial information presented in prescribed forms or schedules that require a prescribed form of auditors' report. (See AU Section 623, *Special Reports.*)

[11]See AU Section 722, *Interim Financial Information.*

processing of transactions by service organizations;[12] and (5) auditing compliance with regulations relating to federal award expenditures and other governmental financial assistance in conjunction with or as a by-product of a financial statement audit.

## Attestation Engagements

1.23 Attestation engagements can cover a broad range of financial or nonfinancial objectives and may provide different levels of assurance about the subject matter or assertion depending on the users' needs. Attestation engagements result in an examination, a review, or an agreed-upon procedures report on a subject matter or on an assertion about a subject matter that is the responsibility of another party. The three types of attestation engagements are:

a. Examination: Consists of obtaining sufficient, appropriate evidence to express an opinion on whether the subject matter is based on (or in conformity with) the criteria in all material respects or the assertion is presented (or fairly stated), in all material respects, based on the criteria.

b. Review: Consists of sufficient testing to express a conclusion about whether any information came to the auditors' attention on the basis of the work performed that indicates the subject matter is not based on (or not in conformity with) the criteria or the assertion is not presented (or not fairly stated) in all material respects based on the criteria. As stated in the AICPA SSAE, auditors should not perform review-level work for reporting on internal control or compliance with laws and regulations.

---

[12]A service organization is the entity or a segment of an entity that provides services to a user organization that are part of the user organization's information system. A user organization is an entity that has engaged a service organization. (See AU Section 324, *Service Organizations*.)

**c.** Agreed-Upon Procedures: Consists of specific procedures performed on a subject matter.

**1.24** The subject matter of an attestation engagement may take many forms. Possible subjects of attestation engagements include reporting on

**a.** prospective financial or performance information;

**b.** management's discussion and analysis (MD&A) presentation;

**c.** an entity's internal control over financial reporting;

**d.** the effectiveness of an entity's internal control over compliance with specified requirements, such as those governing the bidding for, accounting for, and reporting on grants and contracts;

**e.** an entity's compliance with requirements of specified laws, regulations, policies, contracts, or grants;

**f.** the accuracy and reliability of reported performance measures;

**g.** incurred final contract costs are supported with required evidence and in compliance with the contract terms;

**h.** the allowability and reasonableness of proposed contract amounts that are based on detailed costs;

**i.** the quantity, condition, or valuation of inventory or assets; and

**j.** specific procedures performed on a subject matter (agreed-upon procedures).

**Performance Audits**

**1.25** Performance audits are defined as engagements that provide assurance or conclusions based on an evaluation of sufficient, appropriate evidence against stated criteria, such as specific requirements, measures, or defined business practices. Performance audits provide objective analysis so that management and those charged with governance and oversight can use the information to improve program[13] performance and operations, reduce costs, facilitate decision making by parties with responsibility to oversee or initiate corrective action, and contribute to public accountability. Reporting information without following GAGAS is not a performance audit but a nonaudit service provided by an audit organization.

**1.26** Performance audits that comply with GAGAS provide reasonable assurance that the auditors have obtained sufficient, appropriate evidence to support the conclusions reached. Thus, the sufficiency and appropriateness of evidence needed and tests of evidence will vary based on the audit objectives and conclusions.

**1.27** A performance audit is a dynamic process that includes consideration of the applicable standards throughout the course of the audit. An ongoing assessment of the objectives, audit risk, audit procedures, and evidence during the course of the audit facilitates the auditors' determination of what to report and the proper context for the audit conclusions, including discussion about the sufficiency and appropriateness of evidence being used as a basis for the audit conclusions. Performance audit conclusions logically flow from all of these elements and provide an assessment of the audit findings and their implications.

---

[13]The term "program" is used in this document to include government entities, organizations, programs, activities, and functions.

**1.28** Performance audit objectives may vary widely and include assessments of program effectiveness, economy, and efficiency; internal control;[14] compliance; and prospective analyses. These overall objectives are not mutually exclusive. Thus, a performance audit may have more than one overall objective. For example, a performance audit with an initial objective of program effectiveness may also involve an underlying objective of evaluating internal controls to determine the reasons for a program's lack of effectiveness or how effectiveness can be improved.

**1.29** Program effectiveness and results audit objectives are frequently interrelated with economy and efficiency objectives. Audit objectives that focus on program effectiveness and results typically measure the extent to which a program is achieving its goals and objectives. Audit objectives that focus on economy and efficiency address the costs and resources used to achieve program results. Examples of audit objectives in these categories include

**a.** assessing the extent to which legislative, regulatory, or organizational goals and objectives are being achieved;

**b.** assessing the relative ability of alternative approaches to yield better program performance or eliminate factors that inhibit program effectiveness;

---

[14]In the context of performance audits, the term "internal control" in this document is synonymous with the term management control and covers all aspects of an entity's operations (programmatic, financial, and compliance).

c. analyzing the relative cost-effectiveness of a program or activity;[15]

d. determining whether a program produced intended results or produced results that were not consistent with the program's objectives;

e. determining the current status or condition of program operations or progress in implementing legislative requirements;

f. determining whether a program provides equitable access to or distribution of public resources within the context of statutory parameters;

g. assessing the extent to which programs duplicate, overlap, or conflict with other related programs;

h. evaluating whether the audited entity is following sound procurement practices;

i. assessing the reliability, validity, or relevance of performance measures concerning program effectiveness and results, or economy and efficiency;

j. assessing the reliability, validity, or relevance of financial information related to the performance of a program;

k. determining whether government resources (inputs) are obtained at reasonable costs while meeting timeliness and quality considerations;

---

[15]These objectives focus on combining cost information with information about outputs or the benefit provided or with outcomes or the results achieved.

l. determining whether appropriate value was obtained based on the cost or amount paid or based on the amount of revenue received;

m. determining whether government services and benefits are accessible to those individuals who have a right to access those services and benefits;

n. determining whether fees assessed cover costs;

o. determining whether and how the program's unit costs can be decreased or its productivity increased; and

p. assessing the reliability, validity, or relevance of budget proposals or budget requests to assist legislatures in the budget process.

**1.30** Internal control audit objectives relate to an assessment of the component of an organization's system of internal control that is designed to provide reasonable assurance of achieving effective and efficient operations, reliable financial and performance reporting, or compliance with applicable laws and regulations. Internal control objectives also may be relevant when determining the cause of unsatisfactory program performance. Internal control comprises the plans, policies, methods, and procedures used to meet the organization's mission, goals, and objectives. Internal control includes the processes and procedures for planning, organizing, directing, and controlling program operations, and management's system for measuring, reporting, and monitoring program performance. Examples of audit objectives related to internal control include an assessment of the extent to which internal control provides reasonable assurance about whether

a. organizational missions, goals, and objectives are achieved effectively and efficiently;

**b.** resources are used in compliance with laws, regulations, or other requirements;

**c.** resources, including sensitive information accessed or stored outside the organization's physical perimeter, are safeguarded against unauthorized acquisition, use, or disposition;

**d.** management information, such as performance measures, and public reports are complete, accurate, and consistent to support performance and decision making;

**e.** the integrity of information from computerized systems is achieved; and

**f.** contingency planning for information systems provides essential back-up to prevent unwarranted disruption of the activities and functions that the systems support.

**1.31** Compliance audit objectives relate to compliance criteria established by laws, regulations, contract provisions, grant agreements, and other requirements[16] that could affect the acquisition, protection, use, and disposition of the entity's resources and the quantity, quality, timeliness, and cost of services the entity produces and delivers. Compliance objectives include determining whether

**a.** the purpose of the program, the manner in which it is to be conducted, the services delivered, the outcomes, or the population it serves is in compliance with laws, regulations, contract provisions, grant agreements, and other requirements;

---

[16]Compliance requirements can be either financial or nonfinancial.

**b.** government services and benefits are distributed or delivered to citizens based on the individual's eligibility to obtain those services and benefits;

**c.** incurred or proposed costs are in compliance with applicable laws, regulations, and contracts or grant agreements; and

**d.** revenues received are in compliance with applicable laws, regulations, and contract or grant agreements.

**1.32** Prospective analysis audit objectives provide analysis or conclusions, about information that is based on assumptions about events that may occur in the future along with possible actions that the audited entity may take in response to the future events. Examples of objectives pertaining to this work include providing conclusions based on

**a.** current and projected trends and future potential impact on government programs and services;

**b.** program or policy alternatives, including forecasting program outcomes under various assumptions;

**c.** policy or legislative proposals, including advantages, disadvantages, and analysis of stakeholder views;

**d.** prospective information prepared by management;

**e.** budgets and forecasts that are based on
(1) assumptions about expected future events and
(2) management's expected reaction to those future events; and

**f.** management's assumptions on which prospective information is based.

## Professional Services Other Than Audits (Nonaudit Services) Provided by Audit Organizations

**1.33** GAGAS do not cover professional services other than audits or attestation engagements (nonaudit services). (See paragraphs 3.25 through 3.30 for additional discussion of nonaudit services.) Therefore, auditors must not report that the nonaudit services were conducted in accordance with GAGAS. When performing nonaudit services for an entity for which the audit organization performs a GAGAS audit or attestation engagement, audit organizations should communicate, as appropriate, with requestors and those charged with governance to clarify that the scope of work performed does not constitute an audit under GAGAS.

**1.34** Audit organizations that provide nonaudit services must evaluate whether providing nonaudit services creates an independence impairment either in fact or appearance with respect to the entities they audit. (See paragraph 3.02.)

# Chapter 2

# Ethical Principles in Government Auditing

| | |
|---|---|
| **Introduction** | **2.01** Because auditing is essential to government accountability to the public, the public expects audit organizations and auditors who conduct their work in accordance with generally accepted government auditing standards (GAGAS) to follow ethical principles. Management of the audit organization sets the tone for ethical behavior throughout the organization by maintaining an ethical culture, clearly communicating acceptable behavior and expectations to each employee, and creating an environment that reinforces and encourages ethical behavior throughout all levels of the organization. The ethical tone maintained and demonstrated by management and staff is an essential element of a positive ethical environment for the audit organization. |

**2.02** The ethical principles presented in this chapter provide the foundation, discipline, and structure as well as the climate which influence the application of GAGAS. Because the information presented in this chapter deals with fundamental principles rather than specific requirements, this chapter does not contain additional requirements.

**2.03** Conducting audit work in accordance with ethical principles is a matter of personal and organizational responsibility. Ethical principles apply in preserving auditor independence,[17] taking on only work that the auditor is competent to perform, performing high-quality work, and following the applicable standards cited in the audit report. Integrity and objectivity are maintained when auditors perform their work and make decisions that are consistent with the broader interest of those relying on the auditors' report, including the public.

---

[17]Independence requirements are discussed in chapter 3.

## Ethical Principles

**2.04** The ethical principles contained in the following sections provide the overall framework for application of GAGAS, including general standards, field work standards, and reporting standards. Each principle is described, rather than set forth as a series of requirements, so that auditors can consider the facts and circumstances of each situation within the framework of these ethical principles. Other ethical requirements or codes of professional conduct may also be applicable to auditors who conduct audits in accordance with GAGAS. [18]

**2.05** The ethical principles that guide the work of auditors who conduct audits in accordance with GAGAS are

a. the public interest;

b. integrity;

c. objectivity;

d. proper use of government information, resources, and position; and

e. professional behavior.

## The Public Interest

**2.06** The public interest is defined as the collective well-being of the community of people and entities the auditors serve. Observing integrity, objectivity, and independence in discharging their professional

---

[18]Individual auditors who are members of professional organizations or are licensed or certified professionals may also be subject to ethical requirements of those professional organizations or licensing bodies. Auditors in government entities may also be subject to government ethics laws and regulations.

responsibilities assists auditors in meeting the principle of serving the public interest and honoring the public trust. These principles are fundamental to the responsibilities of auditors and critical in the government environment.

**2.07** A distinguishing mark of an auditor is acceptance of responsibility to serve the public interest. This responsibility is critical when auditing in the government environment. GAGAS embody the concept of accountability for public resources, which is fundamental to serving the public interest.

## Integrity

**2.08** Public confidence in government is maintained and strengthened by auditors' performing their professional responsibilities with integrity. Integrity includes auditors' conducting their work with an attitude that is objective, fact-based, nonpartisan, and nonideological with regard to audited entities and users of the auditors' reports. Within the constraints of applicable confidentiality laws, rules, or policies, communications with the audited entity, those charged with governance, and the individuals contracting for or requesting the audit are expected to be honest, candid, and constructive.

**2.09** Making decisions consistent with the public interest of the program or activity under audit is an important part of the principle of integrity. In discharging their professional responsibilities, auditors may encounter conflicting pressures from management of the audited entity, various levels of government, and other likely users. Auditors may also encounter pressures to violate ethical principles to inappropriately achieve personal or organizational gain. In resolving those conflicts and pressures, acting with integrity means that auditors place priority on their responsibilities to the public interest.

## Objectivity

**2.10** The credibility of auditing in the government sector is based on auditors' objectivity in discharging their professional responsibilities. Objectivity includes being independent in fact and appearance when providing audit and attestation engagements, maintaining an attitude of impartiality, having intellectual honesty, and being free of conflicts of interest. Avoiding conflicts that may, in fact or appearance, impair auditors' objectivity in performing the audit or attestation engagement is essential to retaining credibility. Maintaining objectivity includes a continuing assessment of relationships with audited entities and other stakeholders in the context of the auditors' responsibility to the public.[19]

## Proper Use of Government Information, Resources, and Position

**2.11** Government information, resources, or positions are to be used for official purposes and not inappropriately for the auditor's personal gain or in a manner contrary to law or detrimental to the legitimate interests of the audited entity or the audit organization. This concept includes the proper handling of sensitive or classified information or resources.

**2.12** In the government environment, the public's right to the transparency of government information has to be balanced with the proper use of that information. In addition, many government programs are subject to laws and regulations dealing with the disclosure of information. To accomplish this balance, exercising discretion in the use of information acquired in the course of auditors' duties is an important part in achieving this goal. Improperly disclosing any such information to third parties is not an acceptable practice.

---

[19]The concepts of objectivity and independence are very closely related. Problems with independence or conflicts of interest may impair objectivity. (See independence standards at paragraphs 3.02 through 3.30.)

2.13 As accountability professionals, accountability to the public for the proper use and prudent management of government resources is an essential part of auditors' responsibilities. Protecting and conserving government resources and using them appropriately for authorized activities is an important element in the public's expectations for auditors.

2.14 Misusing the position of an auditor for personal gain violates an auditor's fundamental responsibilities. An auditor's credibility can be damaged by actions that could be perceived by an objective third party with knowledge of the relevant information as improperly benefiting an auditor's personal financial interests or those of an immediate or close family member; a general partner; an organization for which the auditor serves as an officer, director, trustee, or employee; or an organization with which the auditor is negotiating concerning future employment. (See paragraphs 3.07 through 3.09 for further discussion of personal impairments to independence.)

## Professional Behavior

2.15 High expectations for the auditing profession include compliance with laws and regulations and avoidance of any conduct that might bring discredit to auditors' work, including actions that would cause an objective third party with knowledge of the relevant information to conclude that the auditors' work was professionally deficient. Professional behavior includes auditors' putting forth an honest effort in performance of their duties and professional services in accordance with the relevant technical and professional standards.

# Chapter 3

# General Standards

## Introduction

**3.01** This chapter establishes general standards and provides guidance for performing financial audits, attestation engagements, and performance audits under generally accepted government auditing standards (GAGAS). (See chapter 6 for an additional general standard applicable only to attestation engagements.) These general standards, along with the overarching ethical principles presented in chapter 2, establish a foundation for credibility of auditors' work. These general standards emphasize the independence of the audit organization and its individual auditors; the exercise of professional judgment in the performance of work and the preparation of related reports; the competence of audit staff; audit quality control and assurance; and external peer reviews.

## Independence

**3.02** In all matters relating to the audit work, the audit organization and the individual auditor, whether government or public, must be free from personal, external, and organizational impairments to independence, and must avoid the appearance of such impairments of independence.

**3.03** Auditors and audit organizations must maintain independence so that their opinions, findings, conclusions, judgments, and recommendations will be impartial and viewed as impartial by objective third parties with knowledge of the relevant information. Auditors should avoid situations that could lead objective third parties with knowledge of the relevant information to conclude that the auditors are not able to maintain independence and thus are not capable of exercising objective and impartial judgment on all issues associated with conducting the audit and reporting on the work.

**3.04** When evaluating whether independence impairments exist either in fact or appearance with respect to the entities for which audit organizations perform audits or attestation engagements, auditors and audit organizations must take into account the three general classes of impairments to independence—personal, external, and organizational.[20] If one or more of these impairments affects or can be perceived to affect independence, the audit organization (or auditor) should decline to perform the work—except in those situations in which an audit organization in a government entity, because of a legislative requirement or for other reasons, cannot decline to perform the work, in which case the government audit organization must disclose the impairment(s) and modify the GAGAS compliance statement. (See paragraphs 1.12 and 1.13.)

**3.05** When auditors use the work of a specialist,[21] auditors should assess the specialist's ability to perform the work and report results impartially as it relates to their relationship with the program or entity under audit. If the specialist's independence is impaired, auditors should not use the work of that specialist.

**3.06** If an impairment to independence is identified after the audit report is issued, the audit organization should assess the impact on the audit. If the audit organization concludes that it did not comply with GAGAS, it should determine the impact on the auditors' report and notify entity management, those charged with governance, the requesters, or regulatory agencies that have jurisdiction over the audited entity and persons known to be using the audit report about the independence impairment and

---

[20]Awareness and compliance with other independence standards and applicable ethics laws and regulations associated with their activities may also be required for auditors performing work in accordance with GAGAS.

[21]Specialists to whom this section applies include, but are not limited to, actuaries, appraisers, attorneys, engineers, environmental consultants, medical professionals, statisticians, and geologists.

the impact on the audit. The audit organization should make such notifications in writing.

## Personal Impairments

**3.07** Auditors participating on an audit assignment must be free from personal impairments to independence.[22] Personal impairments of auditors result from relationships or beliefs that might cause auditors to limit the extent of the inquiry, limit disclosure, or weaken or slant audit findings in any way. Individual auditors should notify the appropriate officials within their audit organizations if they have any personal impairment to independence. Examples of personal impairments of individual auditors include, but are not limited to, the following:

a. immediate family or close family member[23] who is a director or officer of the audited entity, or, as an employee of the audited entity, is in a position to exert direct and significant influence over the entity or the program under audit;

b. financial interest that is direct, or is significant/material though indirect, in the audited entity or program;[24]

---

[22]This includes those who review the work or the report, and all others within the audit organization who can directly influence the outcome of the audit. The period covered includes the period covered by the audit and the period in which the audit is being performed and reported.

[23]Immediate family member is a spouse, spouse equivalent, or dependent (whether or not related). A close family member is a parent, sibling, or nondependent child.

[24]Auditors are not precluded from auditing pension plans that they participate in if (1) the auditor has no control over the investment strategy, benefits, or other management issues associated with the pension plan and (2) the auditor belongs to such pension plan as part of his/her employment with the audit organization, provided that the plan is normally offered to all employees in equivalent employment positions.

c. responsibility for managing an entity or making decisions that could affect operations of the entity or program being audited; for example, serving as a director, officer, or other senior position of the entity, activity, or program being audited, or as a member of management in any decision making, supervisory, or ongoing monitoring function for the entity, activity, or program under audit;

d. concurrent or subsequent performance of an audit by the same individual who maintained the official accounting records when such services involved preparing source documents or originating data, in electronic or other form; posting transactions (whether coded by management or not coded); authorizing, executing, or consummating transactions (for example, approving invoices, payrolls, claims, or other payments of the entity or program being audited); maintaining an entity's bank account or otherwise having custody of the audited entity's funds; or otherwise exercising authority on behalf of the entity, or having authority to do so;

e. preconceived ideas toward individuals, groups, organizations, or objectives of a particular program that could bias the audit;

f. biases, including those resulting from political, ideological, or social convictions that result from membership or employment in, or loyalty to, a particular type of policy, group, organization, or level of government; and

g. seeking employment during the conduct of the audit with an audited organization.

3.08 Audit organizations and auditors may encounter many different circumstances or combinations of circumstances that could create a personal impairment. Therefore, it is impossible to identify every situation that could result in a personal impairment. Accordingly, audit organizations should include as part of their quality control system procedures to identify personal impairments and help ensure compliance with GAGAS independence requirements. At a minimum, audit organizations should

**a.** establish policies and procedures to identify, report, and resolve personal impairments to independence,

**b.** communicate the audit organization's policies and procedures to all auditors in the organization and promote understanding of the policies and procedures,

**c.** establish internal policies and procedures to monitor compliance with the audit organization's policies and procedures,

**d.** establish a disciplinary mechanism to promote compliance with the audit organization's policies and procedures,

**e.** stress the importance of independence and the expectation that auditors will always act in the public interest, and

**f.** maintain documentation of the steps taken to identify potential personal independence impairments.

**3.09** When the audit organization identifies a personal impairment to independence prior to or during an audit, the audit organization should take action to resolve the impairment in a timely manner. In situations in which the personal impairment is applicable only to an individual auditor or a specialist on a particular audit, the audit organization may be able to eliminate the personal impairment. For example, the audit organization could remove that auditor or specialist from any work on that audit or require the auditor or

specialist to eliminate the cause of the personal
impairment. If the personal impairment cannot be
eliminated, the audit organization should withdraw from
the audit. In situations in which auditors employed by
government entities cannot withdraw from the audit,
they should follow paragraph 3.04.

## External Impairments

**3.10** Audit organizations must be free from external
impairments to independence. Factors external to the
audit organization may restrict the work or interfere
with auditors' ability to form independent and objective
opinions, findings, and conclusions. External
impairments to independence occur when auditors are
deterred from acting objectively and exercising
professional skepticism by pressures, actual or
perceived, from management and employees of the
audited entity or oversight organizations. For example,
under the following conditions, auditors may not have
complete freedom to make an independent and
objective judgment, thereby adversely affecting the
audit:

**a.** external interference or influence that could
improperly limit or modify the scope of an audit or
threaten to do so, including exerting pressure to
inappropriately reduce the extent of work performed in
order to reduce costs or fees;

**b.** external interference with the selection or application
of audit procedures or in the selection of transactions to
be examined;

**c.** unreasonable restrictions on the time allowed to
complete an audit or issue the report;

**d.** externally imposed restriction on access to records,
government officials, or other individuals needed to
conduct the audit;

**e.** external interference over the assignment, appointment, compensation, and promotion of audit personnel;

**f.** restrictions on funds or other resources provided to the audit organization that adversely affect the audit organization's ability to carry out its responsibilities;

**g.** authority to overrule or to inappropriately influence the auditors' judgment as to the appropriate content of the report;

**h.** threat of replacing the auditors over a disagreement with the contents of an audit report, the auditors' conclusions, or the application of an accounting principle or other criteria; and

**i.** influences that jeopardize the auditors' continued employment for reasons other than incompetence, misconduct, or the need for audits or attestation engagements.

**3.11** Audit organizations should include policies and procedures for identifying and resolving external impairments as part of their quality control system for compliance with GAGAS independence requirements.

## Organizational Independence

**3.12** The ability of audit organizations in government entities to perform work and report the results objectively can be affected by placement within government, and the structure of the government entity being audited. Whether reporting to third parties externally or to top management within the audited entity internally, audit organizations must be free from organizational impairments to independence with respect to the entities they audit. Impairments to organizational independence result when the audit function is organizationally located within the reporting line of the areas under audit or when the auditor is assigned or takes on responsibilities that affect operations of the area under audit.

**Organizational Independence for External Audit Organizations**

**3.13** External audit organizations can be presumed to be free from organizational impairments to independence when the audit function is organizationally placed outside the reporting line of the entity under audit and the auditor is not responsible for entity operations. Audit organizations in government entities can meet the requirement for organizational independence in a number of ways and may be presumed to be free from organizational impairments to independence from the audited entity if the audit organization is

a. at a level of government other than the one to which the audited entity is assigned (federal, state, or local); for example, federal auditors auditing a state government program; or

b. in a different branch of government within the same level of government as the audited entity; for example, legislative auditors auditing an executive branch program.

**3.14** Audit organizations in government entities may also be presumed to be free from organizational impairments if the head of the audit organization meets any of the following criteria:

a. directly elected by voters of the jurisdiction being audited;

b. elected or appointed by a legislative body, subject to removal by a legislative body, and reports the results of audits to and is accountable to a legislative body;

c. appointed by someone other than a legislative body, so long as the appointment is confirmed by a legislative body and removal from the position is subject to oversight or approval by a legislative body,[25] and reports the results of audits to and is accountable to a legislative body; or

**d.** appointed by, accountable to, reports to, and can only be removed by a statutorily created governing body, the majority of whose members are independently elected or appointed and come from outside the organization being audited.

**3.15** In addition to the presumptive criteria in paragraphs 3.13 and 3.14, GAGAS recognize that there may be other organizational structures under which audit organizations in government entities could be considered to be free from organizational impairments and thereby be considered organizationally independent for reporting externally. These structures provide safeguards to prevent the audited entity from interfering with the audit organization's ability to perform the work and report the results impartially. For an external audit organization to be considered free from organizational impairments under a structure different from the ones listed in paragraphs 3.13 and 3.14, the audit organization should have all of the following safeguards. In such situations, the audit organization should document how each of the following safeguards were satisfied and provide the documentation to those performing quality control monitoring and to the external peer reviewers to determine whether all the necessary safeguards have been met.

---

[25]Legislative bodies may exercise their confirmation powers through a variety of means so long as they are involved in the approval of the individual to head the audit organization. This involvement can be demonstrated by approving the individual after the appointment or by initially selecting or nominating an individual or individuals for appointment by the appropriate authority.

**a.** statutory protections that prevent the audited entity from abolishing the audit organization;

**b.** statutory protections that require that if the head of the audit organization is removed from office, the head of the agency report this fact and the reasons for the removal to the legislative body;

**c.** statutory protections that prevent the audited entity from interfering with the initiation, scope, timing, and completion of any audit;

**d.** statutory protections that prevent the audited entity from interfering with audit reporting, including the findings and conclusions or the manner, means, or timing of the audit organization's reports;

**e.** statutory protections that require the audit organization to report to a legislative body or other independent governing body on a recurring basis;

**f.** statutory protections that give the audit organization sole authority over the selection, retention, advancement, and dismissal of its staff; and

**g.** statutory access to records and documents related to the agency, program, or function being audited and access to government officials or other individuals as needed to conduct the audit.[26]

**Organizational Independence for Internal Audit Functions**

**3.16** Certain federal, state, or local government entities employ auditors to work for management of the audited entities. These auditors may be subject to administrative direction from persons involved in the entity management process. Such audit organizations are

---

[26]Statutory authority to issue a subpoena to obtain the needed records is one way to meet the requirement for statutory access to records.

internal audit functions and are en⌐
Institute of Internal Auditors (IIA) *I           ⌐ʋnal
Standards for the Professional Practice of Internal
Auditing* in conjunction with GAGAS. Under GAGAS, a
government internal audit function can be presumed to
be free from organizational impairments to
independence for reporting internally if the head of the
audit organization meets all of the following criteria:

**a.** is accountable to the head or deputy head of the
government entity or to those charged with governance;

**b.** reports the audit results both to the head or deputy
head of the government entity and to those charged with
governance;

**c.** is located organizationally outside the staff or line-
management function of the unit under audit;

**d.** has access to those charged with governance; and

**e.** is sufficiently removed from political pressures to
conduct audits and report findings, opinions, and
conclusions objectively without fear of political reprisal.

**3.17** The internal audit organization should report
regularly to those charged with governance.

**3.18** When internal audit organizations that are free of
organizational impairments perform audits of external
parties such as auditing contractors or outside party
agreements, and no personal or external impairments
exist, they may be considered independent of the
audited entities and free to report objectively to the
heads or deputy heads of the government entities to
which they are assigned, to those charged with
governance, and to parties outside the organizations in
accordance with applicable law, rule, regulation, or
policy.

**3.19** The internal audit organization should document the conditions that allow it to be considered free of organizational impairments to independence for internal reporting and provide the documentation to those performing quality control monitoring and to the external peer reviewers to determine whether all the necessary safeguards have been met.

Organizational
Independence When
Performing Nonaudit
Services

**3.20** Audit organizations at times may perform other professional services (nonaudit services) that are not performed in accordance with GAGAS. Audit organizations that provide nonaudit services must evaluate whether providing the services creates an independence impairment either in fact or appearance with respect to entities they audit.[27] Based on the facts and circumstances, professional judgment is used in determining whether a nonaudit service would impair an audit organization's independence with respect to entities it audits.

**3.21** Audit organizations in government entities generally have broad audit responsibilities and, therefore, should establish policies and procedures for accepting engagements to perform nonaudit services so that independence is not impaired with respect to entities they audit. (See appendix I, paragraphs A3.02 and A3.03 for examples of nonaudit services that are generally specific to audit organizations in government entities that generally do not impair the organizations' independence with respect to the entities it audits and, therefore, do not require compliance with the supplemental safeguards described in paragraph 3.30.)

---

[27]The Government Accountability Office (GAO) has issued further guidance in the form of questions and answers to assist in implementation of the standards associated with nonaudit services. This guidance, *Government Auditing Standards: Answers to Independence Standard Questions*, GAO-02-870G (Washington, D.C.: June 2002), can be found on GAO's Government Auditing Standards Web page (http://www.gao.gov/govaud/ybk01.htm).

Independent public accountants may provide audit and nonaudit services (commonly referred to as consulting) under contractual commitments to an entity and should determine whether nonaudit services they have provided or are committed to provide have a significant or material effect on the subject matter of the audits.

## Overarching Independence Principles

**3.22** The following two overarching principles apply to auditor independence when assessing the impact of performing a nonaudit service for an audited program or entity: (1) audit organizations must not provide nonaudit services that involve performing management functions or making management decisions and (2) audit organizations must not audit their own work or provide nonaudit services in situations in which the nonaudit services are significant or material to the subject matter of the audits.[28]

**3.23** In considering whether audits performed by the audit organization could be significantly or materially affected by the nonaudit service, audit organizations should evaluate (1) ongoing audits; (2) planned audits; (3) requirements and commitments for providing audits, which includes laws, regulations, rules, contracts, and other agreements; and (4) policies placing responsibilities on the audit organization for providing audit services.

**3.24** If requested[29] to perform nonaudit services that would impair the audit organization's ability to meet either or both of the overarching independence

---

[28] The concepts of significance and materiality include quantitative as well as qualitative measures in relation to the subject matter of the audit.

[29] The requestor of nonaudit services could be the management of the audited entity or a third party such as a legislative oversight body.

principles for certain types of audit work, the audit organization should inform the requestor and the audited entity that performing the nonaudit service would impair the auditors' independence with regard to subsequent audit or attestation engagements.

## Types of Nonaudit Services

**3.25** Nonaudit services generally fall into one of the following categories (see appendix I, paragraphs A3.02 and A3.03 for examples of nonaudit services that are generally unique to audit organizations in government entities):

**a.** Nonaudit services that do not impair the audit organization's independence with respect to the entities it audits and, therefore, do not require compliance with the supplemental safeguards in paragraph 3.30. (See paragraphs 3.26 and 3.27.)

**b.** Nonaudit services that would not impair the audit organization's independence with respect to the entities it audits as long as the audit organization complies with the supplemental safeguards in paragraph 3.30. (See paragraph 3.28.)

**c.** Nonaudit services that do impair the audit organization's independence. Compliance with the supplemental safeguards will not overcome this impairment. (See paragraph 3.29.)

### Nonaudit Services That Do Not Impair Auditor Independence

**3.26** Nonaudit services in which auditors provide technical advice based on their technical knowledge and expertise do not impair auditor independence with respect to entities they audit and do not require the audit organization to apply the supplemental safeguards.

However, auditor independence would be impaired if the extent or nature of the advice resulted in the auditors' making management decisions or performing management functions.

**3.27** Examples of the types of services considered as providing technical advice include the following:

**a.** participating in activities such as commissions, committees, task forces, panels, and focus groups as an expert in a purely advisory, nonvoting capacity to

**(1)** advise entity management on issues based on the auditors' knowledge or

**(2)** address urgent problems;

**b.** providing tools and methodologies, such as guidance and good business practices, benchmarking studies, and internal control assessment methodologies that can be used by management; and

**c.** providing targeted and limited technical advice to the audited entity and management to assist them in activities such as (1) answering technical questions or providing training, (2) implementing audit recommendations, (3) implementing internal controls, and (4) providing information on good business practices.

### Nonaudit Services That Would Not Impair Independence if Supplemental Safeguards Are Implemented

**3.28** Services that do not impair the audit organization's independence with respect to the entities they audit so long as they comply with supplemental safeguards include the following:

**a.** providing basic accounting assistance limited to services such as preparing draft financial statements that are based on management's chart of accounts and trial balance and any adjusting, correcting, and closing entries that have been approved by management; preparing draft notes to the financial statements based on information determined and approved by management; preparing a trial balance based on management's chart of accounts; maintaining depreciation schedules for which management has determined the method of depreciation, rate of depreciation, and salvage value of the asset (If the audit organization has prepared draft financial statements and notes and performed the financial statement audit, the auditor should obtain documentation from management in which management acknowledges the audit organization's role in preparing the financial statements and related notes and management's review, approval, and responsibility for the financial statements and related notes in the management representation letter. The management representation letter that is obtained as part of the audit may be used for this type of documentation.);

**b.** providing payroll services when payroll is not material to the subject matter of the audit or to the audit objectives. Such services are limited to using records and data that have been approved by entity management;

**c.** providing appraisal or valuation services limited to services such as reviewing the work of the entity or a specialist employed by the entity where the entity or specialist provides the primary evidence for the balances recorded in financial statements or other information that will be audited; valuing an entity's pension, other post-employment benefits, or similar liabilities provided management has determined and taken responsibility for all significant assumptions and data;

**d.** preparing an entity's indirect cost proposal[30] or cost allocation plan provided that the amounts are not material to the financial statements and management assumes responsibility for all significant assumptions and data;

**e.** providing advisory services on information technology limited to services such as advising on system design, system installation, and system security if management, in addition to the safeguards in paragraph 3.30, acknowledges responsibility for the design, installation, and internal control over the entity's system and does not rely on the auditors' work as the primary basis for determining (1) whether to implement a new system, (2) the adequacy of the new system design, (3) the adequacy of major design changes to an existing system, and (4) the adequacy of the system to comply with regulatory or other requirements;

**f.** providing human resource services to assist management in its evaluation of potential candidates when the services are limited to activities such as serving on an evaluation panel of at least three individuals to review applications or interviewing candidates to provide input to management in arriving at a listing of best qualified applicants to be provided to management; and

**g.** preparing routine tax filings based on information provided by the audited entity.

---

[30]The Office of Management and Budget (OMB) prohibits an auditor who prepared the entity's indirect cost proposal from conducting the required audit when indirect costs recovered by the entity during the prior year exceeded $1 million under OMB Circular No. A-133, *Audits of States, Local Governments, and Non-Profit Organizations*, Subpart C.305(b), revised June 27, 2003.

## Nonaudit Services That Impair Independence

**3.29** Compliance with supplemental safeguards will not overcome independence impairments in this category. By their nature, certain nonaudit services directly support the entity's operations and impair the audit organization's ability to meet either or both of the overarching independence principles in paragraph 3.22 for certain types of audit work. Examples of the types of services under this category include the following:

**a.** maintaining or preparing the audited entity's basic accounting records or maintaining or taking responsibility for basic financial or other records that the audit organization will audit;

**b.** posting transactions (whether coded or not coded) to the entity's financial records or to other records that subsequently provide input to the entity's financial records;

**c.** determining account balances or determining capitalization criteria;

**d.** designing, developing, installing, or operating the entity's accounting system or other information systems that are material or significant to the subject matter of the audit;

**e.** providing payroll services that (1) are material to the subject matter of the audit or the audit objectives, and/or (2) involve making management decisions;

**f.** providing appraisal or valuation services that exceed the scope described in paragraph 3.28 c;

**g.** recommending a single individual for a specific position that is key to the entity or program under audit, otherwise ranking or influencing management's selection of the candidate, or conducting an executive search or a recruiting program for the audited entity;

h. developing an entity's performance measurement system when that system is material or significant to the subject matter of the audit;

i. developing an entity's policies, procedures, and internal controls;

j. performing management's assessment of internal controls when those controls are significant to the subject matter of the audit;

k. providing services that are intended to be used as management's primary basis for making decisions that are significant to the subject matter under audit;

l. carrying out internal audit functions, when performed by external auditors; and

m. serving as voting members of an entity's management committee or board of directors, making policy decisions that affect future direction and operation of an entity's programs, supervising entity employees, developing programmatic policy, authorizing an entity's transactions, or maintaining custody of an entity's assets.[31]

## Supplemental Safeguards for Maintaining Auditor Independence When Performing Nonaudit Services

**3.30** Performing nonaudit services described in paragraph 3.28 will not impair independence if the

---

[31]Entity assets are intended to include all of the entity's property including bank accounts, investment accounts, inventories, equipment, or other assets owned, leased, or otherwise in the entity's possession, and financial records, both paper and electronic.

overarching independence principles stated in paragraph 3.22 are not violated. For these nonaudit services, the audit organization should comply with each of the following safeguards:

**a.** document its consideration of the nonaudit services, including its conclusions about the impact on independence;

**b.** establish in writing an understanding with the audited entity regarding the objectives, scope of work, and product or deliverables of the nonaudit service; and management's responsibility for (1) the subject matter of the nonaudit services, (2) the substantive outcomes of the work, and (3) making any decisions that involve management functions related to the nonaudit service and accepting full responsibility for such decisions;

**c.** exclude personnel who provided the nonaudit services from planning, conducting, or reviewing audit work in the subject matter of the nonaudit service;[32] and

**d.** do not reduce the scope and extent of the audit work below the level that would be appropriate if the nonaudit service were performed by an unrelated party.

## Professional Judgment

**3.31** Auditors must use professional judgment in planning and performing audits and attestation engagements and in reporting the results.

**3.32** Professional judgment includes exercising reasonable care and professional skepticism. Reasonable care concerns acting diligently in

---

[32]Personnel who provided the nonaudit service are permitted to convey to the audit team the documentation and knowledge gained about the audited entity and its operations.

accordance with applicable professional standards and ethical principles. Professional skepticism is an attitude that includes a questioning mind and a critical assessment of evidence. Professional skepticism includes a mindset in which auditors assume neither that management is dishonest nor of unquestioned honesty. Believing that management is honest is not a reason to accept less than sufficient, appropriate evidence.

**3.33** Using the auditors' professional knowledge, skills, and experience to diligently perform, in good faith and with integrity, the gathering of information and the objective evaluation of the sufficiency and appropriateness of evidence is a critical component of audits. Professional judgment and competence are interrelated because judgments made are dependent upon the auditors' competence.

**3.34** Professional judgment represents the application of the collective knowledge, skills, and experiences of all the personnel involved with an assignment, as well as the professional judgment of individual auditors. In addition to personnel directly involved in the audit, professional judgment may involve collaboration with other stakeholders, outside experts, and management in the audit organization.

**3.35** Using professional judgment in all aspects of carrying out their professional responsibilities, including following the independence standards, maintaining objectivity and credibility, assigning competent audit staff to the assignment, defining the scope of work, evaluating and reporting the results of the work, and maintaining appropriate quality control over the assignment process is essential to performing and reporting on an audit.

**3.36** Using professional judgment is important in determining the required level of understanding of the audit subject matter and related circumstances. This includes consideration about whether the audit team's collective experience, training, knowledge, skills, abilities, and overall understanding are sufficient to assess the risks that the subject matter under audit may contain a significant inaccuracy or could be misinterpreted.

**3.37** Considering the risk level of each assignment, including the risk that they may come to an improper conclusion is another important issue. Within the context of audit risk, exercising professional judgment in determining the sufficiency and appropriateness of evidence to be used to support the findings and conclusions based on the audit objectives and any recommendations reported is an integral part of the audit process.

**3.38** Auditors should document significant decisions affecting the audit objectives, scope, and methodology; findings; conclusions; and recommendations resulting from professional judgment.

**3.39** While this standard places responsibility on each auditor and audit organization to exercise professional judgment in planning and performing an audit or attestation engagement, it does not imply unlimited responsibility, nor does it imply infallibility on the part of either the individual auditor or the audit organization. Absolute assurance is not attainable because of the nature of evidence and the characteristics of fraud. Professional judgment does not mean eliminating all possible limitations or weaknesses associated with a specific audit, but rather identifying, considering, minimizing, mitigating, and explaining them.

## Competence

**3.40** The staff assigned to perform the audit or attestation engagement must collectively possess adequate professional competence for the tasks required.

**3.41** The audit organization's management should assess skill needs to consider whether its workforce has the essential skills that match those necessary to fulfill a particular audit mandate or scope of audits to be performed. Accordingly, audit organizations should have a process for recruitment, hiring, continuous development, assignment, and evaluation of staff to maintain a competent workforce. The nature, extent, and formality of the process will depend on various factors such as the size of the audit organization, its structure, and its work.

**3.42** Competence is derived from a blending of education and experience. Competencies are not necessarily measured by years of auditing experience because such a quantitative measurement may not accurately reflect the kinds of experiences gained by an auditor in any given time period. Maintaining competence through a commitment to learning and development throughout an auditor's professional life is an important element for auditors. Competence enables an auditor to make sound professional judgments.

## Technical Knowledge and Competence

**3.43** The staff assigned to conduct an audit or attestation engagement under GAGAS must collectively possess the technical knowledge, skills, and experience necessary to be competent for the type of work being performed before beginning work on that assignment. The staff assigned to a GAGAS audit or attestation engagement should collectively possess

**a.** knowledge of GAGAS applicable to the type of work they are assigned and the education, skills, and experience to apply this knowledge to the work being performed;

**b.** general knowledge of the environment in which the audited entity operates and the subject matter under review;

**c.** skills to communicate clearly and effectively, both orally and in writing; and

**d.** skills appropriate for the work being performed. For example, staff or specialist skills in

**(1)** statistical sampling if the work involves use of statistical sampling;

**(2)** information technology if the work involves review of information systems;

**(3)** engineering if the work involves review of complex engineering data;

**(4)** specialized audit methodologies or analytical techniques, such as the use of complex survey instruments, actuarial-based estimates, or statistical analysis tests, as applicable; or

**(5)** specialized knowledge in subject matters, such as scientific, medical, environmental, educational, or any other specialized subject matter, if the work calls for such expertise.

Additional Qualifications for Financial Audits and Attestation Engagements

**3.44** Auditors performing financial audits should be knowledgeable in generally accepted accounting principles (GAAP), the American Institute of Certified Public Accountants (AICPA) generally accepted auditing standards for field work and reporting and the related Statements on Auditing Standards (SAS), and the application of these standards. Also, if auditors use GAGAS in conjunction with any other standards, they should be knowledgeable and competent in applying those standards. Auditors engaged to perform financial audits or attestation engagements should be licensed certified public accountants or persons working for a licensed certified public accounting firm or a government auditing organization.[33]

**3.45** Similarly, for attestation engagements, GAGAS incorporate the AICPA attestation standards. Auditors should be knowledgeable in the AICPA general attestation standard related to criteria, the AICPA attestation standards for field work and reporting, and the related Statements on Standards for Attestation Engagements (SSAE), and they should be competent in applying these standards and SSAE to the task assigned. Also, if auditors use GAGAS in conjunction with any other standards, they should be knowledgeable and competent in applying those standards.

## Continuing Professional Education

**3.46** Auditors performing work under GAGAS, including planning, directing, performing field work, or reporting on an audit or attestation engagement under GAGAS, should maintain their professional competence through continuing professional education (CPE). Therefore, each auditor performing work under GAGAS should complete, every 2 years, at least 24 hours of CPE that directly relates to government auditing, the government environment, or the specific or unique environment in which the audited entity operates. For auditors who are involved in any amount of planning, directing, or reporting on GAGAS assignments and those auditors who are not involved in those activities but charge 20

---

[33]Public accountants licensed on or before December 31, 1970, or persons working for a public accounting firm licensed on or before December 31, 1970, are also considered qualified under this standard.

percent or more of their time annually to GAGAS assignments should also obtain at least an additional 56 hours of CPE (for a total of 80 hours of CPE in every 2- year period) that enhances the auditor's professional proficiency to perform audits or attestation engagements. Auditors required to take the total 80 hours of CPE should complete at least 20 hours of CPE in each year of the 2-year period.

**3.47** CPE programs are structured educational activities with learning objectives designed to maintain or enhance participants' knowledge, skills, and abilities in areas applicable to performing audits or attestation engagements. Determining what subjects are appropriate for individual auditors to satisfy both the 80-hour and the 24-hour requirements is a matter of professional judgment to be exercised by auditors in consultation with appropriate officials in their audit organizations. Among the considerations in exercising that judgment are the auditors' experience, the responsibilities they assume in performing GAGAS assignments, and the operating environment of the audited entity.

**3.48** Improving their own competencies and meeting CPE requirements are primarily the responsibilities of individual auditors. The audit organization should have quality control procedures to help ensure that auditors meet the continuing education requirements, including documentation of the CPE completed. The Government Accountability Office (GAO) has developed guidance pertaining to CPE requirements to assist auditors and audit organizations in exercising professional judgment in complying with the CPE requirements.[34]

---

[34]This guidance, *Government Auditing Standards: Guidance on GAGAS Requirements for Continuing Professional Education*, GAO-05-568G (Washington, D.C.: April 2005), can be found on GAO's Government Auditing Standards Web page (http://www.gao.gov/govaud/ybk01.htm).

**3.49** External specialists assisting in performing a GAGAS assignment should be qualified and maintain professional competence in their areas of specialization but are not required to meet the GAGAS CPE requirements described. However, auditors who use the work of external specialists should assess the professional qualifications of such specialists and document their findings and conclusions. Internal specialists who are part of the audit organization and perform as a member of the audit team should comply with GAGAS, including the CPE requirements.

## Quality Control and Assurance

**3.50** Each audit organization performing audits or attestation engagements in accordance with GAGAS must:

**a.** establish a system of quality control that is designed to provide the audit organization with reasonable assurance that the organization and its personnel comply with professional standards and applicable legal and regulatory requirements, and

**b.** have an external peer review at least once every 3 years.[35]

## System of Quality Control

**3.51** An audit organization's system of quality control encompasses the audit organization's leadership, emphasis on performing high quality work, and the organization's policies and procedures designed to

---

[35]An audit organization's noncompliance with the peer review requirements (paragraph 3.50b and 3.55 through 3.60) results in a modified GAGAS compliance statement. The audit organization's compliance (or noncompliance) with the requirements for a system of quality control in paragraphs 3.50a and 3.51 through 3.54 are tested and reported on as part of the peer review process and do not impact the GAGAS compliance statement. (See chapter 1, paragraphs 1.11 through 1.13.)

provide reasonable assurance of complying with
professional standards and applicable legal and
regulatory requirements.[36] The nature, extent, and
formality of an audit organization's quality control
system will vary based on the audit organization's
circumstances, such as the audit organization's size,
number of offices and geographic dispersion, the
knowledge and experience of its personnel, the nature
and complexity of its audit work, and cost-benefit
considerations.

**3.52** Each audit organization must document its quality
control policies and procedures and communicate those
policies and procedures to its personnel. The audit
organization should document compliance with its
quality control policies and procedures and maintain
such documentation for a period of time sufficient to
enable those performing monitoring procedures and
peer reviews to evaluate the extent of the audit
organization's compliance with its quality control
policies and procedures. The form and content of such
documentation are a matter of professional judgment
and will vary based on the audit organization's
circumstances.

**3.53** An audit organization should include policies and
procedures in its system of quality control that
collectively address:

**a.** Leadership responsibilities for quality within the audit
organization: Policies and procedures that designate
responsibility for quality of audits and attestation
engagements performed under GAGAS and

---

[36]The system of quality control discussed in this section is consistent
with the AICPA proposed statement on Quality Control Standards, *A
Firm's System of Quality Control*, except that the GAGAS
requirements in paragraph 3.54 state that reviews of the work and the
report that are performed as part of supervision are not monitoring
controls when used alone.

communication of policies and procedures relating to quality. Such policies and communications encourage a culture that recognizes that quality is essential in performing GAGAS audits.

**b.** Independence, legal, and ethical requirements: Policies and procedures designed to provide reasonable assurance that the audit organization and its personnel maintain independence, and comply with applicable legal and ethical requirements.[37]

**c.** Initiation,[38] acceptance, and continuance of audit and attestation engagements: Policies and procedures for the initiation, acceptance, and continuance of audit and attestation engagements, designed to provide reasonable assurance that the audit organization will undertake audit engagements only if it can comply with professional standards and ethical principles and is acting within the legal mandate or authority of the audit organization.

**d.** Human resources: Policies and procedures designed to provide the audit organization with reasonable assurance that it has personnel with the capabilities and competence to perform its audits in accordance with

---

[37]See paragraphs 3.02 through 3.30 for GAGAS dealing with independence. See chapter 2 for GAGAS ethical principles. Individual auditors who are members of professional organizations or are licensed or certified professionals may also be subject to ethical requirements of those professional organizations or licensing bodies. Auditors in government entities may also be subject to government ethics laws and regulations.

[38]Government audit organizations initiate audit and attestation engagements as a result of (1) the audit organization's discretion, (2) requests from legislative bodies or oversight bodies, and (3) legal mandates. In the case of requests and legal mandates, a government audit organization may be required to do the work. See paragraph 3.04 for requirements where an audit organization in a government entity is not independent and, because of a legislative requirement or for other reasons, cannot decline to perform the work.

professional standards and legal and regulatory requirements.[39]

**e.** Audit and attestation engagement performance, documentation, and reporting: Policies and procedures designed to provide the audit organization with reasonable assurance that audits and attestation engagements are performed and reports are issued in accordance with professional standards and legal and regulatory requirements. (For financial audits, chapters 1 through 5 apply; for attestation engagements, chapters 1 through 3 and 6 apply; for performance audits, chapters 1 through 3 and 7 and 8 apply.)

**f.** Monitoring of quality: An ongoing, periodic assessment of work completed on audits and attestation engagements designed to provide management of the audit organization with reasonable assurance that the policies and procedures related to the system of quality control are suitably designed and operating effectively in practice. The purpose of monitoring compliance with quality control policies and procedures is to provide an evaluation of (1) adherence to professional standards and legal and regulatory requirements, (2) whether the quality control system has been appropriately designed, and (3) whether quality control policies and procedures are operating effectively and complied with in practice. Monitoring procedures will vary based on the audit organization's facts and circumstances. The audit organization should perform monitoring procedures that enable it to assess compliance with applicable professional standards and quality control policies and procedures for GAGAS audits. Individuals performing monitoring should collectively have sufficient expertise and authority for this role.

---

[39]See paragraphs 3.40 through 3.49 for requirements dealing with professional competence.

**3.54** The audit organization should analyze and summarize the results of its monitoring procedures at least annually, with identification of any systemic issues needing improvement, along with recommendations for corrective action. (Under GAGAS, reviews of the work and the report that are performed as part of supervision are not monitoring controls when used alone. However, these types of pre-issuance reviews may be used as a part of this analysis and summary.)

## External Peer Review

**3.55** Audit organizations performing audits and attestation engagements in accordance with GAGAS must have an external peer review performed by reviewers independent of the audit organization being reviewed at least once every 3 years.[40]

**3.56** The audit organization should obtain an external peer review sufficient in scope to provide a reasonable basis for determining whether, for the period under review,[41] the reviewed audit organization's system of quality control was suitably designed and whether the audit organization is complying with its quality control system in order to provide the audit organization with reasonable assurance of conforming with applicable professional standards.

**3.57** The peer review team should include the following elements in the scope of the peer review:

---

[40]The external peer review requirement is effective within 3 years from the date an audit organization begins field work on its first assignment in accordance with GAGAS for both financial audit practices and performance audit practices. Generally, the deadlines for peer review reports are established by the entity that administers the peer review program. Extensions of the deadlines for submitting the peer review report exceeding 3 months beyond the due date are granted by the entity that administers the peer review program and GAO.

[41]The period under review generally covers 1 year. Peer review programs and audit organizations may choose a longer period to be covered by the peer review.

**a.** review of the audit organization's quality control policies and procedures;

**b.** consideration of the adequacy and results of the audit organization's internal monitoring procedures;

**c.** review of selected audit and attestation engagement reports and related documentation;

**d.** review of other documents necessary for assessing compliance with standards, for example, independence documentation, CPE records, and relevant human resource management files; and

**e.** interviews with a selection of the reviewed audit organization's professional staff at various levels to assess their understanding of and compliance with relevant quality control policies and procedures.

**3.58** The peer review team should perform a risk assessment to help determine the number and types of engagements to select. Based on the risk assessment, the team should use one or a combination of the following approaches to selecting individual audits and attestation engagements for review: (1) select GAGAS audits and attestation engagements that provide a reasonable cross-section of the GAGAS assignments performed by the reviewed audit organization or (2) select audits and attestation engagements that provide a reasonable cross-section from all types of work subject to the reviewed audit organization's quality control system, including one or more assignments performed in accordance with GAGAS.[42]

---

[42]The second approach is generally applicable to audit organizations that perform only a small number of GAGAS audits in relation to other types of audits. In these cases, one or more GAGAS audits may represent more than what would be selected when looking at a cross-section of the audit organization's work as a whole.

**3.59** The peer review team should prepare one or more written reports communicating the results of the peer review, including the following:

**a.** description of the scope of the peer review, including any limitations;

**b.** an opinion on whether the system of quality control of the reviewed audit organization's audit and/or attestation engagement practices was adequately designed and complied with during the period reviewed to provide the audit organization with reasonable assurance of conforming with applicable professional standards;

**c.** specification of the professional standards to which the reviewed audit organization is being held;

**d.** for modified or adverse opinions,[43] a description of reasons for the modification or adverse opinion, along with a detailed description of the findings and recommendations, in the peer review report, to enable the reviewed audit organization to take appropriate actions; and

**e.** reference to a separate letter of comments, if such a letter is issued.

**3.60** The peer review team should meet the following criteria:

---

[43]A modified opinion is an opinion in which the peer reviewer concludes that except for the effects of deficiencies described in the eport, the system of quality control was adequately designed and complied with during the period. An adverse opinion is a conclusion that the system of quality control was not adequately designed and complied with to provide reasonable assurance of conforming with professional standards.

**a.** The review team collectively has current knowledge of GAGAS and government auditing.

**b.** The organization conducting the peer review and individual review team members are independent (as defined in GAGAS) of the audit organization being reviewed, its staff, and the audits and attestation engagements selected for the peer review.

**c.** The review team collectively has sufficient knowledge of how to perform a peer review. Such knowledge may be obtained from on-the-job training, training courses, or a combination of both. Having personnel on the peer review team with prior experience on a peer review or internal inspection team is desirable.

**3.61** An external audit organization[44] should make its most recent peer review report[45] publicly available; for example, by posting the peer review report on an external Web site or to a publicly available file designed for public transparency of peer review results. If neither of these options is available to the audit organization, then it should use the same transparency mechanism it uses to make other information public, and also provide the peer review report to others upon request. Internal audit organizations that report internally to management should provide a copy of the external peer review report to those charged with governance. Government audit organizations should also communicate the overall results and the availability of their external peer review reports to appropriate oversight bodies.

**3.62** Information in external peer review reports and letters of comment may be relevant to decisions on

---

[44]An external audit organization is defined in paragraphs 3.13 through 3.15.

[45]This requirement does not include the letter of comment.

procuring audit or attestation engagements. Therefore, audit organizations seeking to enter into a contract to perform an audit or attestation engagement in accordance with GAGAS should provide the following to the party contracting for such services:

**a.** the audit organization's most recent peer review report and any letter of comment, and

**b.** any subsequent peer review reports and letters of comment received during the period of the contract.

**3.63** Auditors who are using another audit organization's work should request a copy of the audit organization's latest peer review report and any letter of comment, and the audit organization should provide these documents when requested. (See paragraphs 3.05 and 7.41 through 7.43 for further requirements and guidance on using the work of others.)

# Chapter 4

# Field Work Standards for Financial Audits

Introduction

**4.01** This chapter establishes field work standards and provides guidance for financial audits conducted in accordance with generally accepted government auditing standards (GAGAS). This chapter identifies the American Institute of Certified Public Accountants (AICPA) field work standards and prescribes additional standards for financial audits performed in accordance with GAGAS.

**a.** For financial audits, GAGAS incorporate the AICPA field work and reporting standards and the related statements on auditing standards (SAS) unless specifically excluded or modified by GAGAS.[46]

**b.** Under AICPA standards and GAGAS, auditors must plan and perform the audit to obtain sufficient appropriate audit evidence so that audit risk will be limited to a low level that is, in their professional judgment, appropriate for expressing an opinion on the financial statements. The high, but not absolute, level of assurance that is intended to be obtained by auditors is expressed in the auditor's report as obtaining reasonable assurance about whether the financial statements are free of material misstatement (whether caused by error or fraud). Absolute assurance is not attainable because of the nature of audit evidence and the characteristics of fraud. Therefore, an audit conducted in accordance with generally accepted auditing standards may not detect a material misstatement.

**4.02** For financial audits performed in accordance with GAGAS, chapters 1 through 5 apply.

---

[46]To date, the Comptroller General has not excluded any field work standards or SAS.

## AICPA Field Work Standards

**4.03** The three AICPA generally accepted standards of field work are as follows:[47]

**a.** The auditor must adequately plan the work and must properly supervise any assistants.

**b.** The auditor must obtain a sufficient understanding of the entity and its environment, including its internal control, to assess the risk of material misstatement of the financial statements whether due to error or fraud, and to design the nature, timing, and extent of further audit procedures.

**c.** The auditor must obtain sufficient appropriate audit evidence by performing audit procedures to afford a reasonable basis for an opinion regarding the financial statements under audit.

## Additional Government Auditing Standards

**4.04** GAGAS establish field work standards for financial audits in addition to the requirements contained in the AICPA standards. Auditors should comply with these additional standards when citing GAGAS in their audit reports. The additional government auditing standards relate to:

**a.** auditor communication during planning (see paragraphs 4.05 through 4.08);

**b.** previous audits and attestation engagements (see paragraph 4.09);

**c.** detecting material misstatements resulting from violations of provisions of contracts or grant

---

[47]See AU Section 150, *Generally Accepted Auditing Standards.*

agreements, or from abuse (see paragraphs 4.10 through 4.13);

**d.** developing elements of a finding (see paragraphs 4.14 through 4.18); and

**e.** audit documentation (see paragraphs 4.19 through 4.24).

## Auditor Communication During Planning

**4.05** Under AICPA standards and GAGAS, auditors should communicate with the audited entity their understanding of the services to be performed for each engagement and document that understanding through a written communication.[48] GAGAS broaden the parties included in the communication and the items for the auditors to communicate.

**4.06** Under GAGAS, when planning the audit, auditors should communicate certain information in writing to management of the audited entity, those charged with governance,[49] and to the individuals contracting for or requesting the audit. When auditors perform the audit pursuant to a law or regulation or they conduct the work for the legislative committee that has oversight of the audited entity, auditors should communicate with the legislative committee. In those situations where there is not a single individual or group that both oversees the strategic direction of the entity and the fulfillment of its accountability obligations or in other situations where the identity of those charged with governance is not clearly evident, auditors should document the process

---

[48]See AICPA Statement on Auditing Standard No. 108, *Planning and Supervision.*

[49]Those charged with governance are those responsible for overseeing the strategic direction of the entity and the entity's fulfillment of its obligations related to the accountability of the entity. (See appendix I, paragraphs A1.05 through A1.07 for additional information.)

followed and conclusions reached for identifying the
appropriate individuals to receive the required auditor
communications. Auditors should communicate the
following additional information under GAGAS:

**a**. The nature of planned work and level of assurance to
be provided related to internal control over financial
reporting and compliance with laws, regulations, and
provisions of contracts or grant agreements.

**b**. Any potential restriction on the auditors' reports, in
order to reduce the risk that the needs or expectations
of the parties involved may be misinterpreted.

**4.07** Under AICPA standards and GAGAS, tests of
internal control over financial reporting and compliance
with laws, regulations, and provisions of contracts or
grant agreements in a financial statement audit
contribute to the evidence supporting the auditors'
opinion on the financial statements or other conclusions
regarding financial data. However, such tests generally
are not sufficient in scope to provide an opinion on the
effectiveness of internal control over financial reporting
or compliance with laws, regulations, and provisions of
contracts or grant agreements. To meet the needs of
certain audit report users, laws and regulations
sometimes prescribe supplemental testing and reporting
on internal control over financial reporting and

compliance with laws, regulations, and provisions of contracts and grant agreements.[50]

**4.08** If an audit is terminated before it is completed and an audit report is not issued, auditors should document the results of the work to the date of termination and why the audit was terminated. Determining whether and how to communicate the reason for terminating the audit to those charged with governance, appropriate officials of the audited entity, the entity contracting for or requesting the audit, and other appropriate officials will depend on the facts and circumstances and, therefore, is a matter of professional judgment.

## Previous Audits and Attestation Engagements

**4.09** Auditors should evaluate whether the audited entity has taken appropriate corrective action to address findings and recommendations from previous engagements that could have a material effect on the financial statements. When planning the audit, auditors should ask management of the audited entity to identify previous audits, attestation engagements, and other studies that directly relate to the objectives of the audit, including whether related recommendations have been implemented. Auditors should use this information in assessing risk and determining the nature, timing, and extent of current audit work, including determining the extent to which testing the implementation of the

---

[50]For example, when engaged to perform audits under the Single Audit Act, as amended, for state and local government entities and nonprofit entities that receive federal awards, auditors follow Office of Management and Budget (OMB) Circular No. A-133. The act and circular include specific audit requirements, mainly in the areas of compliance with laws and regulations and internal control over compliance that go beyond the requirements in chapters 4 and 5 of GAGAS. Audits performed pursuant to the Chief Financial Officers Act of 1990, as expanded by the Government Management Reform Act of 1994 and the Accountability of Tax Dollars Act of 2002, also have specific audit requirements prescribed by OMB in the areas of internal control and compliance. In addition, some state and local governments may have additional audit requirements that the auditors would need to follow in planning the audit.

corrective actions is applicable to the current audit
objectives.

## Detecting Material Misstatements Resulting from Violations of Provisions of Contracts or Grant Agreements or from Abuse

**4.10** Auditors should design the audit to provide
reasonable assurance of detecting misstatements that
result from violations of provisions of contracts or grant
agreements and could have a direct and material effect
on the determination of financial statement amounts or
other financial data significant to the audit objectives.

**4.11** If specific information comes to the auditors'
attention that provides evidence concerning the
existence of possible violations of provisions of
contracts or grant agreements that could have a material
indirect effect on the financial statements, the auditors
should apply audit procedures specifically directed to
ascertaining whether such violations have occurred.
When the auditors conclude that a violation of
provisions of contracts or grant agreements has or is
likely to have occurred, they should determine the effect
on the financial statements as well as the implications
for other aspects of the audit.

**4.12** Abuse involves behavior that is deficient or
improper when compared with behavior that a prudent
person would consider reasonable and necessary
business practice given the facts and circumstances.
Abuse also includes misuse of authority or position for
personal financial interests or those of an immediate or
close family member or business associate. Abuse does
not necessarily involve fraud, violation of laws,
regulations, or provisions of a contract or grant
agreement.

**4.13** If during the course of the audit, auditors become
aware of abuse that could be quantitatively or
qualitatively material to the financial statements,
auditors should apply audit procedures specifically

directed to ascertain the potential effect on the financial statements or other financial data significant to the audit objectives. After performing additional work, auditors may discover that the abuse represents potential fraud or illegal acts. Because the determination of abuse is subjective, auditors are not required to provide reasonable assurance of detecting abuse.

## Developing Elements of a Finding

**4.14** Audit findings may involve deficiencies in internal control, fraud, illegal acts, violations of provisions of contracts or grant agreements, and abuse. The elements needed for a finding depend entirely on the objectives of the audit. Thus, a finding or set of findings is complete to the extent that the audit objectives are satisfied. When auditors identify deficiencies, auditors should plan and perform procedures to develop the elements of the findings that are relevant and necessary to achieve the audit objectives. The elements of an audit finding are discussed in paragraphs 4.15 through 4.18.

**4.15** Criteria: The laws, regulations, contracts, grant agreements, standards, measures, expected performance, defined business practices, and benchmarks against which performance is compared or evaluated. Criteria identify the required or desired state or expectation with respect to the program or operation. Criteria provide a context for evaluating evidence and understanding the findings.

**4.16** Condition: Condition is a situation that exists. The condition is determined and documented during the audit.

**4.17** Cause: The cause identifies the reason or explanation for the condition or the factor or factors responsible for the difference between the situation that exists (condition) and the required or desired state (criteria), which may also serve as a basis for recommendations for corrective actions. Common factors include poorly designed policies, procedures, or criteria; inconsistent, incomplete, or incorrect implementation; or factors beyond the control of program management. Auditors may assess whether the evidence provides a reasonable and convincing argument for why the stated cause is the key factor or factors contributing to the difference.

**4.18** Effect or potential effect: The effect is a clear, logical link to establish the impact or potential impact of the difference between the situation that exists (condition) and the required or desired state (criteria). The effect or potential effect identifies the outcomes or consequences of the condition. When the audit objectives include identifying the actual or potential consequences of a condition that varies (either positively or negatively) from the criteria identified in the audit, "effect" is a measure of those consequences. Effect or potential effect may be used to demonstrate the need for corrective action in response to identified problems or relevant risks.

## Audit Documentation

**4.19** Under AICPA standards and GAGAS, auditors must prepare audit documentation in connection with each audit in sufficient detail to provide a clear understanding of the work performed (including the nature, timing, extent, and results of audit procedures performed), the audit evidence obtained and its source, and the conclusions reached.[51] Under AICPA standards and GAGAS, auditors should prepare audit documentation

---

[51]See AU Section 339.03 for the AICPA standard on audit documentation.

that enables an experienced auditor,[52] having no
previous connection to the audit, to understand

**a.** the nature, timing, and extent of auditing procedures
performed to comply with GAGAS and other applicable
standards and requirements;

**b.** the results of the audit procedures performed and the
audit evidence obtained;

**c.** the conclusions reached on significant matters; and

**d.** that the accounting records agree or reconcile with
the audited financial statements or other audited
information.

**4.20** Under GAGAS, auditors also should document,
before the audit report is issued, evidence of supervisory
review of the work performed that supports findings,
conclusions, and recommendations contained in the
audit report.

**4.21** When auditors do not comply with applicable
GAGAS requirements due to law, regulation, scope
limitations, restrictions on access to records, or other
issues impacting the audit, the auditors should
document the departure from the GAGAS requirements
and the impact on the audit and on the auditors'
conclusions. This applies to departures from both
mandatory requirements and presumptively mandatory
requirements where alternative procedures performed

---

[52]An experienced auditor means an individual (whether internal or
external to the audit organization) who possesses the competencies
and skills that would have enabled him or her to perform the audit.
These competencies and skills include an understanding of (1) audit
processes, (2) GAGAS and applicable legal and regulatory
requirements, (3) the environment in which the entity operates, and
(4) auditing and financial reporting issues relevant to the audited
entity's environment.

in the circumstances were not sufficient to achieve the objectives of the standard. (See paragraphs 1.12 and 1.13.)

**4.22** Audit organizations should establish policies and procedures for the safe custody and retention of audit documentation for a time sufficient to satisfy legal, regulatory, and administrative requirements for record retention. Whether audit documentation is in paper, electronic, or other media, the integrity, accessibility, and retrievability of the underlying information could be compromised if the documentation is altered, added to, or deleted without the auditors' knowledge, or if the documentation is lost or damaged. For audit documentation that is retained electronically, the audit organization should establish information systems controls concerning accessing and updating the audit documentation.

**4.23** Underlying GAGAS audits is the premise that audit organizations in federal, state, and local governments and public accounting firms engaged to perform a financial audit in accordance with GAGAS cooperate in auditing programs of common interest so that auditors may use others' work and avoid duplication of efforts. Subject to applicable laws and regulations, auditors should make appropriate individuals, as well as audit documentation, available upon request and in a timely manner to other auditors or reviewers to satisfy these objectives. The use of auditors' work by other auditors may be facilitated by contractual arrangements for GAGAS audits that provide for full and timely access to appropriate individuals, as well as audit documentation.

**4.24** Audit organizations should develop policies to deal with requests by outside parties to obtain access to audit documentation, especially when an outside party attempts to obtain information indirectly through the auditor rather than directly from the audited entity. In

developing such policies, audit organizations should
determine what laws and regulations apply, if any.

## Additional Considerations for GAGAS Financial Audits

**4.25** Due to the audit objectives and public
accountability of GAGAS audits, there may be additional
considerations for financial audits completed in
accordance with GAGAS. These considerations relate to

**a.** materiality in GAGAS financial audits (see paragraph
4.26);

**b.** consideration of fraud and illegal acts (see
paragraphs 4.27 and 4.28); and

**c.** ongoing investigations or legal proceedings (see
paragraph 4.29).

## Materiality in GAGAS Financial Audits

**4.26** Under both AICPA standards and GAGAS, the
auditors' responsibility is to plan and perform the audit
to obtain reasonable assurance that material
misstatements, whether caused by errors or fraud, are
detected.[53] The concept of materiality recognizes that
some matters, either individually or in the aggregate, are
important for fair presentation of financial statements in
conformity with generally accepted accounting
principles, while other matters are not important. In
performing the audit, matters that, either individually or
in the aggregate, could be material to the financial
statements are a primary consideration.[54] Additional
considerations may apply to GAGAS financial audits of
government entities or entities that receive government

---

[53]See AU Section 110, *Responsibilities and Functions of the
Independent Auditor.*

[54]See AICPA Statement on Auditing Standards No. 107, *Audit Risk and
Materiality in Conducting an Audit.*

awards. For example, in audits performed in accordance with GAGAS, auditors may find it appropriate to use lower materiality levels as compared with the materiality levels used in non-GAGAS audits because of the public accountability of government entities and entities receiving government funding, various legal and regulatory requirements, and the visibility and sensitivity of government programs.[55]

## Consideration of Fraud and Illegal Acts

**4.27** Under both the AICPA standards[56] and GAGAS, auditors should plan and perform the audit to obtain reasonable assurance about whether the financial statements are free of material misstatement, whether caused by error or fraud.[57] Recognizing the possibility that a material misstatement due to fraud could be present is important for achieving this objective. However, absolute assurance is not attainable and thus even a properly planned and performed audit may not detect a material misstatement resulting from fraud.

---

[55]In accordance with AICPA Statement on Auditing Standards No. 107, *Audit Risk and Materiality in Conducting an Audit,* the auditor's consideration of materiality is a matter of professional judgment and is influenced by the auditor's perception of the needs of users of financial statements. The Financial Accounting Standards Board defined materiality in its Statement of Financial Accounting Concepts No. 2, *Qualitative Characteristics of Accounting Information* as "the magnitude of an omission or misstatement of accounting information that, in the light of surrounding circumstances, makes it probable that the judgment of a reasonable person relying on the information would have been changed or influenced by the omission or misstatement."

[56]See AU Section 316, *Consideration of Fraud in a Financial Statement Audit.*

[57]Two types of misstatements are relevant to the auditors' consideration of fraud in an audit of financial statements– misstatements arising from fraudulent financial reporting and misstatements arising from misappropriation of assets. The primary factor that distinguishes fraud from error is whether the underlying action that results in the misstatement in the financial statements is intentional or unintentional.

**4.28** Under both the AICPA standards[58] and GAGAS, auditors should design the audit to provide reasonable assurance of detecting material misstatements resulting from illegal acts that could have a direct and material effect on the financial statements.[59] If specific information comes to the auditors' attention that provides evidence concerning the existence of possible illegal acts[60] that could have a material indirect effect on the financial statements, the auditors should apply audit procedures specifically directed to ascertaining whether an illegal act has occurred. When an illegal act has or is likely to have occurred, auditors should determine the effect on the financial statements as well as the implications for other aspects of the audit.

## Ongoing Investigations or Legal Proceedings

**4.29** Avoiding interference with investigations or legal proceedings is important in pursuing indications of fraud, illegal acts, violations of provisions of contracts or grant agreements, or abuse. Laws, regulations, or policies might require auditors to report indications of certain types of fraud, illegal acts, violations of provisions of contracts or grant agreements, or abuse to law enforcement or investigatory authorities before performing additional audit procedures. When investigations or legal proceedings are initiated or in

---

[58]See AU Sections 317.02, 317.05, and 316.01 for AICPA standards and guidance related to auditors' responsibilities when a possible illegal act is detected.

[59]Illegal acts are violations of laws or government regulations that have a direct and material effect on the determination of financial statement amounts. For example, applicable laws and regulations may affect the amount of revenue accrued under government contracts. However, the auditor considers such laws or regulations from the perspective of their known relation to audit objectives derived from financial statement assertions rather than from the perspective of legality per se.

[60]Whether a particular act is, in fact, illegal may have to await final determination by a court of law or other adjudicative body. Disclosing matters that have led auditors to conclude that an illegal act is likely to have occurred is not a final determination of illegality.

process, auditors should evaluate the impact on the current audit. In some cases, it may be appropriate for the auditors to work with investigators and/or legal authorities, or withdraw from or defer further work on the audit engagement or a portion of the engagement to avoid interfering with an investigation.

# Chapter 5

# Reporting Standards for Financial Audits

## Introduction

**5.01** This chapter establishes reporting standards and provides guidance for financial audits conducted in accordance with generally accepted government auditing standards (GAGAS). For financial audits, GAGAS incorporate the American Institute of Certified Public Accountants (AICPA) field work and reporting standards and the related statements on auditing standards (SAS) unless specifically excluded or modified by GAGAS.[61] This chapter identifies the AICPA reporting standards and prescribes additional standards for financial audits performed in accordance with GAGAS.

**5.02** For financial audits performed in accordance with GAGAS, chapters 1 through 5 apply.

## AICPA Reporting Standards

**5.03** The four AICPA generally accepted standards of reporting[62] are as follows:

**a.** The auditor must state in the auditor's report whether the financial statements are presented in accordance with generally accepted accounting principles (GAAP).

**b.** The auditor must identify in the auditor's report those circumstances in which such principles have not been consistently observed in the current period in relation to the preceding period.

---

[61]To date, the Comptroller General has not excluded any reporting standards or SAS.

[62]See AU Section 150, *Generally Accepted Auditing Standards*. Under AU Section 150, when an auditor reports on financial statements prepared in accordance with a comprehensive basis of accounting other than GAAP, the first standard of reporting is satisfied by stating in the auditor's report that the basis of presentation is a comprehensive basis of accounting other than GAAP and by expressing an opinion (or disclaiming an opinion) on whether the financial statements are presented in conformity with the comprehensive basis of accounting used.

**c.** When the auditor determines that informative disclosures are not reasonably adequate, the auditor must so state in the auditor's report.

**d.** The auditor must either express an opinion regarding the financial statements, taken as a whole, or state that an opinion cannot be expressed, in the auditor's report. When the auditor cannot express an overall opinion, the auditor should state the reasons therefor in the auditor's report. In all cases where an auditor's name is associated with financial statements, the auditor should clearly indicate the character of the auditor's work, if any, and the degree of responsibility the auditor is taking in the auditor's report.

## Additional Government Auditing Standards

**5.04** GAGAS establish reporting standards for financial audits in addition to the standards contained in the AICPA standards. Auditors should comply with these additional standards when citing GAGAS in their audit reports. The additional government auditing standards relate to

**a.** reporting auditors' compliance with GAGAS (see paragraphs 5.05 and 5.06);

**b.** reporting on internal control and compliance with laws, regulations, and provisions of contracts or grant agreements (see paragraphs 5.07 through 5.09);

**c.** reporting deficiencies in internal control, fraud, illegal acts, violations of provisions of contracts or grant agreements, and abuse (see paragraphs 5.10 through 5.22);

**d.** communicating significant matters in the auditors' report (see paragraphs 5.23 through 5.25);

**e.** reporting on the restatement of previously-issued financial statements (see paragraphs 5.26 through 5.31);

**f.** reporting views of responsible officials (see paragraphs 5.32 through 5.38);

**g.** reporting confidential or sensitive information (see paragraphs 5.39 through 5.43); and

**h.** distributing reports (see paragraph 5.44).

## Reporting Auditors' Compliance with GAGAS

**5.05** When auditors comply with all applicable GAGAS requirements, they should include a statement in the auditors' report that they performed the audit in accordance with GAGAS. (See paragraphs 1.12 and 1.13 for additional requirements on citing compliance with GAGAS.)

**5.06** An audited entity receiving a GAGAS audit report may also request auditors to issue a financial audit report for purposes other than complying with requirements for a GAGAS audit. For example, the audited entity may need audited financial statements to issue bonds or for other financing purposes. GAGAS do not prohibit auditors from issuing a separate report conforming only to AICPA or other standards.

## Reporting on Internal Control and Compliance with Laws, Regulations, and Provisions of Contracts or Grant Agreements

**5.07** When providing an opinion or a disclaimer on financial statements, auditors must also report on internal control over financial reporting and on compliance with laws, regulations, and provisions of contracts or grant agreements.

**5.08** Auditors should include either in the same or in separate report(s) a description of the scope of the auditors' testing of internal control over financial reporting and compliance with laws, regulations, and provisions of contracts or grant agreements. If the auditors issue separate reports, they should include a reference to the separate reports in the report on financial statements. Auditors should state in the reports whether the tests they performed provided sufficient, appropriate evidence to support an opinion on the effectiveness of internal control over financial reporting and on compliance with laws, regulations, and provisions of contracts or grant agreements. The internal control reporting standard under GAGAS differs from the objective of an examination of internal control in accordance with the AICPA Statement on Standards for Attestation Engagements (SSAE), which is to express an opinion on the design or the design and operating effectiveness of an entity's internal control, as applicable. To form a basis for expressing such an opinion, the auditor must plan and perform the examination to obtain reasonable assurance about whether the entity maintained, in all material respects, effective internal control as of a point in time or for a specified period of time.

**5.09** When auditors report separately (including separate reports bound in the same document) on internal control over financial reporting and compliance with laws and regulations and provisions of contracts or grant agreements, they should state in the financial statement audit report that they are issuing those additional reports. They should include a reference to the separate reports[63] and also state that the reports on internal control over financial reporting and compliance with laws and regulations and provisions of contracts or grant agreements are an integral part of a GAGAS audit and important for assessing the results of the audit. If auditors issued or intend to issue a management letter,

---

[63]This requirement applies to financial statement audits described in paragraph 1.22a. It does not apply to other types of financial audits described in paragraph 1.22b.

they should refer to that management letter in the reports.

## Reporting Deficiencies in Internal Control, Fraud, Illegal Acts, Violations of Provisions of Contracts or Grant Agreements, and Abuse

**5.10** For financial audits, including audits of financial statements in which auditors provide an opinion or disclaimer, auditors should report, as applicable to the objectives of the audit, and based upon the audit work performed, (1) significant deficiencies in internal control, identifying those considered to be material weaknesses; (2) all instances of fraud and illegal acts unless inconsequential; and (3) violations of provisions of contracts or grant agreements and abuse that could have a material effect on the financial statements.[64]

## Deficiencies in Internal Control

**5.11** For all financial audits, auditors should report the following deficiencies in internal control:

**a.** Significant deficiency: a deficiency in internal control, or combination of deficiencies, that adversely affects the entity's ability to initiate, authorize, record, process, or report financial data reliably in accordance with GAAP such that there is more than a remote[65] likelihood that a misstatement of the entity's financial statements that is

---

[64]If the auditor is performing an audit in accordance with Office of Management and Budget (OMB) Circular No. A-133, *Audits of States, Local Governments, and Non-Profit Organizations,* the thresholds for reporting are defined in the circular. Those reporting thresholds satisfy GAGAS.

[65]The term "more than remote" used in the definitions for significant deficiency and material weakness means "at least reasonably possible." The following definitions apply: (1) Remote—The chance of the future events occurring is slight. (2) Reasonably possible—The chance of the future events or their occurrence is more than remote but less than likely. (3) Probable—The future events are likely to occur.

more than inconsequential[66] will not be prevented or detected.[67]

**b.** Material weakness: a significant deficiency, or combination of significant deficiencies, that results in more than a remote likelihood that a material misstatement of the financial statements will not be prevented or detected.

**5.12** Assessing the significance of control deficiencies includes qualitative considerations such as public accountability of the audited entity, legal and regulatory requirements, the visibility and sensitivity of the entity or program, the needs of users and concerns of oversight officials, and current and emerging risks and uncertainties facing the government entity or entity that receives government funding. The significance of a deficiency in internal control also is influenced by

**a.** the likelihood that a deficiency, or combination of deficiencies, could fail to prevent or detect a material misstatement of an account balance or disclosure; and

**b.** the magnitude of the potential misstatement.

---

[66]The phrase "more than inconsequential" as used in the definition of significant deficiency describes the magnitude of potential misstatement that could occur as a result of a significant deficiency and serves as a threshold for evaluating whether a control deficiency or combination of control deficiencies is a significant deficiency. A misstatement is inconsequential if a reasonable person would conclude, after considering the possibility of further undetected misstatements, that the misstatement, either individually or when aggregated with other misstatements, would clearly be immaterial to the financial statements. If a reasonable person would not reach such a conclusion regarding a particular misstatement, that misstatement is more than inconsequential.

[67]See appendix I, paragraph A.04 for examples of control deficiencies. AU Section 325, *Communicating Internal Control Related Matters Identified in an Audit*, also provides guidance on evaluating potential control deficiencies and examples.

**5.13** Auditors should include all significant deficiencies in the auditors' report on internal control over financial reporting and indicate those that represent material weaknesses. If (1) a significant deficiency is remediated before the auditors' report is issued and (2) the auditors obtain sufficient, appropriate evidence supporting the remediation of the significant deficiency, then the auditors should report the significant deficiency and the fact that it was remediated before the auditors' report was issued.

**5.14** Determining whether and how to communicate to officials of the audited entity internal control deficiencies that have an inconsequential effect on the financial statements is a matter of professional judgment. Auditors should document such communications.

## Fraud, Illegal Acts, Violations of Provisions of Contracts or Grant Agreements, and Abuse

**5.15** Under AICPA standards and GAGAS, auditors have responsibilities for detecting fraud and illegal acts that have a material effect on the financial statements and determining whether those charged with governance are adequately informed about fraud and illegal acts. GAGAS include additional reporting standards. When auditors conclude, based on sufficient, appropriate evidence, that any of the following either has occurred or is likely to have occurred, they should include in their audit report the relevant information about

**a.** fraud and illegal acts[68] that have an effect on the financial statements that is more than inconsequential,

**b.** violations of provisions of contracts or grant agreements that have a material effect on the

---

[68]Whether a particular act is, in fact, illegal may have to await final determination by a court of law or other adjudicative body. Disclosing matters that have led auditors to conclude that an illegal act is likely to have occurred is not a final determination of illegality.

determination of financial statement amounts or other financial data significant to the audit, and

c. abuse that is material, either quantitatively or qualitatively. (See paragraphs 4.12 and 4.13 for a discussion of abuse.)

**5.16** When auditors detect violations of provisions of contracts or grant agreements or abuse that have an effect on the financial statements that is less than material but more than inconsequential, they should communicate those findings in writing to officials of the audited entity. Determining whether and how to communicate to officials of the audited entity fraud, illegal acts, violations of provisions of contracts or grant agreements, or abuse that is inconsequential is a matter of professional judgment. Auditors should document such communications.

**5.17** When fraud, illegal acts, violations of provisions of contracts or grant agreements, or abuse either have occurred or are likely to have occurred, auditors may consult with authorities or legal counsel about whether publicly reporting such information would compromise investigative or legal proceedings. Auditors may limit their public reporting to matters that would not compromise those proceedings, and for example, report only on information that is already a part of the public record.

**Reporting Findings Directly to Parties Outside the Audited Entity**

**5.18** Auditors should report known or likely fraud, illegal acts, violations of provisions of contracts or grant agreements, or abuse directly to parties outside the audited entity in the following two circumstances.[69]

---

[69]Internal audit organizations do not have a duty to report outside the entity unless required by law, rule, regulation, or policy. (See paragraph 5.44b for reporting standards for internal audit organizations when reporting externally.)

**a.** When entity management fails to satisfy legal or regulatory requirements to report such information to external parties specified in law or regulation, auditors should first communicate the failure to report such information to those charged with governance. If the audited entity still does not report this information to the specified external parties as soon as practicable after the auditors' communication with those charged with governance, then the auditors should report the information directly to the specified external parties.

**b.** When entity management fails to take timely and appropriate steps to respond to known or likely fraud, illegal acts, violations of provisions of contracts or grant agreements, or abuse that (1) is likely to have a material effect on the financial statements and (2) involves funding received directly or indirectly from a government agency, auditors should first report management's failure to take timely and appropriate steps to those charged with governance. If the audited entity still does not take timely and appropriate steps as soon as practicable after the auditors' communication with those charged with governance, then the auditors should report the entity's failure to take timely and appropriate steps directly to the funding agency.

**5.19** The reporting in paragraph 5.18 is in addition to any legal requirements to report such information directly to parties outside the audited entity. Auditors should comply with these requirements even if they have resigned or been dismissed from the audit prior to its completion.

**5.20** Auditors should obtain sufficient, appropriate evidence, such as confirmation from outside parties, to corroborate assertions by management of the audited entity that it has reported such findings in accordance with laws, regulations, and funding agreements. When auditors are unable to do so, they should report such information directly as discussed in paragraph 5.18.

## Presenting Findings in the Auditors' Report

**5.21** In presenting findings such as deficiencies in internal control, fraud, illegal acts, violations of provisions of contracts or grant agreements, and abuse, auditors should develop the elements of the findings to the extent necessary to achieve the audit objectives. Clearly developed audit findings, as discussed in paragraphs 4.14 through 4.18, assist management or oversight officials of the audited entity in understanding the need for taking corrective action. If auditors sufficiently develop the elements of a finding, they may provide recommendations for corrective action.

**5.22** Auditors should place their findings in perspective by describing the nature and extent of the issues being reported and the extent of the work performed that resulted in the finding. To give the reader a basis for judging the prevalence and consequences of these findings, auditors should, as applicable, relate the instances identified to the population or the number of cases examined and quantify the results in terms of dollar value or other measures, as appropriate. If the results cannot be projected, auditors should limit their conclusions appropriately.

## Communicating Significant Matters in the Auditors' Report

**5.23** Under AICPA standards, auditors may emphasize in the auditors' report significant matters regarding the financial statements.[70] Due to the public interest in the operations of government entities and entities that receive or administer government awards, there may be situations in GAGAS audits in which certain types of information would help facilitate the readers'

---

[70]AU Section 508.19 establishes standards and provides guidance on emphasis of a matter in an auditors' report.

understanding of the financial statements and the auditors' report. These situations may be in addition to the examples presented in AICPA standards.

**5.24** Examples of matters that auditors may communicate in a GAGAS audit include the following:

**a.** Significant concerns or uncertainties about the fiscal sustainability of a government or program or other matters that could have a significant impact on the financial condition or operations of the government entity beyond 1 year of the financial statement date.[71] Such concerns or uncertainties may arise due to revenue or expenditure trends; economic dependency on other governments or entities; the government's current commitments, responsibilities, liabilities, or promises to citizens for future benefits that are not sustainable over the long term; deficit trends; the relationship between the financial information and other key indicators; and other significant risks and uncertainties that raise doubts about the long-term sustainability of current government programs in relation to the resources expected to be available. However, auditors are not responsible for designing audit procedures to detect such concerns or uncertainties, and any judgment about the future is based on information that is available at the time the judgment is made.

**b.** Unusual or catastrophic events that will likely have a significant ongoing or future impact on the entity's financial condition or operations.

---

[71]AU Section 341, *The Auditor's Consideration of an Entity's Ability to Continue as a Going Concern,* establishes standards and provides guidance on auditor responsibilities with regard to an entity's ability to continue as a going concern for a reasonable period of time, not to exceed 1 year beyond the date of the financial statements being audited.

**c.** Significant uncertainties surrounding projections or estimations in the financial statements.

**d.** Any other matter that the auditors consider significant for communication to users and oversight bodies in the auditors' report.

**5.25** Determining whether to communicate such information in the auditors' report is a matter of professional judgment. The communication may be presented in a separate paragraph or separate section of the auditors' report and may include information that is not disclosed in the financial statements.

## Reporting on Restatement of Previously-Issued Financial Statements

**5.26** AICPA Professional Standards, AU Section 561, *Subsequent Discovery of Facts Existing at the Date of the Auditor's Report*, establish standards and provide guidance for situations when auditors become aware of new information that could have affected their report on previously-issued financial statements.[72] Under AU Section 561, if auditors become aware of new information that might have affected their opinion on previously-issued financial statement(s), then the auditors should advise entity management to determine the potential effect(s) of the new information on the previously-issued financial statement(s) as soon as reasonably possible. Such new information may lead management to conclude that previously-issued financial statements were materially misstated and to restate and reissue the misstated financial statements. In such circumstances, auditors should advise management to make appropriate disclosure of the newly discovered facts and their impact on the financial

---

[72]AU Section 420, *Consistency of Application of GAAP*, and AU Section 508, *Reports on Audited Financial Statements*, provide guidance on when to reissue auditors' reports on restated financial statements.

statements to those who are likely to rely on the financial statements.[73]

**5.27** Under GAGAS, auditors should advise management to make appropriate disclosures when the auditors believe that the following conditions exist: (1) it is likely that previously-issued financial statements are misstated and (2) the misstatement is or reasonably could be material. Under GAGAS, auditors also should perform the following procedures related to restated financial statements:[74]

**a.** evaluate the timeliness and appropriateness of management's disclosure and actions to determine and correct misstatements in previously-issued financial statements (see paragraph 5.28),

**b.** report on restated financial statements (see paragraphs 5.29 and 5.30), and

**c.** report directly to appropriate officials when the audited entity does not take the necessary steps (see paragraph 5.31).

Evaluate the Timeliness and Appropriateness of Management's Disclosure and Actions to Determine and Correct Misstatements in Previously-Issued Financial Statements

**5.28** Auditors should evaluate the timeliness and appropriateness of management's disclosure to those who are likely to rely on the financial statements and management's actions to determine and correct misstatements in previously-issued financial statements in accordance with AU Sections 561.06 through 561.08. Under GAGAS, auditors also should evaluate whether management

---

[73]In GAGAS audits, those likely to rely on the financial statements include, at a minimum, those charged with governance, appropriate oversight bodies, and funding agencies.

[74]These additional GAGAS requirements also apply to other financial information on which auditors opine, such as schedules of expenditures of federal awards.

**a.** acted in an appropriate time frame after new information was available to (1) determine the financial statement effects of the new information and (2) notify those who are likely to rely on the financial statements;

**b.** disclosed the nature and extent of the known or likely material misstatements on Web pages where management has published the auditors' report on the previously-issued financial statements; and

**c.** disclosed the following information in the entity's restated financial statements: (1) the nature and cause(s) of the misstatement(s) that led to the need for restatement, (2) the specific amount(s) of the material misstatement(s), and (3) the related effect(s) on the previously-issued financial statement(s) (e.g., year(s) being restated, specific financial statement(s) affected and line items restated, actions the agency's management took after discovering the misstatement), and (4) the impact on the financial statements as a whole (e.g., change in overall net position, change in the audit opinion) and on key information included in the Management Discussion & Analysis.

## Report on Restated Financial Statements

**5.29** When management restates financial statements, auditors should perform audit procedures sufficient to reissue or update the auditors' report on the restated financial statements regardless of whether the restated financial statements are separately issued or presented on a comparative basis with those of a subsequent period.[75] Auditors should include the following in an explanatory paragraph in the reissued or updated auditors' report:

---

[75]AU Section 9561.02 provides guidance on auditor association with subsequently discovered information when the auditor has resigned or been discharged. AU Sections 508.70 through 508.73 discusses reissuing predecessor auditors' reports.

**a.** a statement disclosing that the previously-issued financial statements have been restated;

**b.** a statement that (1) the previously-issued auditors' report (identified by report date) is not to be relied on because the previously-issued financial statements were materially misstated and (2) the previously-issued auditors' report is replaced by the auditors' report on the restated financial statements;

**c.** a reference to the note(s) to the restated financial statements that discusses the restatement; and

**d**. if applicable, a reference to the report on internal control containing a discussion of any significant internal control deficiency identified by the auditors as having failed to prevent or detect the misstatement and any corrective action taken by management to address the deficiency.

**5.30** Management's failure to include appropriate disclosures, as discussed in paragraph 5.28c, in restated financial statements may have implications for the audit. In addition, auditors should include the omitted disclosures in the auditors' report, if practicable.

Report Directly to Appropriate Officials When the Audited Entity Does Not Take the Necessary Steps

**5.31** Auditors should notify those charged with governance if entity management (1) does not act in an appropriate time frame after new information was available to determine the financial statement effects of the new information and take the necessary steps to timely inform those who are likely to rely on the financial statements and the related auditors' reports of the situation or (2) does not restate with reasonable timeliness the financial statements under circumstances in which auditors believe they need to be restated. Auditors should inform those charged with governance that the auditors will take steps to prevent further reliance on the auditors' report and advise them to notify oversight bodies and funding agencies that rely on the financial statements. If those charged with governance do not notify appropriate oversight bodies and funding agencies, then the auditors should do so.[76]

## Reporting Views of Responsible Officials

**5.32** If the auditors' report discloses deficiencies in internal control, fraud, illegal acts, violations of provisions of contracts or grant agreements, or abuse, auditors should obtain and report the views of responsible officials concerning the findings, conclusions, and recommendations, as well as planned corrective actions.

**5.33** Providing a draft report with findings for review and comment by responsible officials of the audited entity and others helps the auditors develop a report that is fair, complete, and objective. Including the views of responsible officials results in a report that presents not only the auditors' findings, conclusions, and recommendations, but also the perspectives of the responsible officials of the audited entity and the corrective actions they plan to take. Obtaining the comments in writing is preferred, but oral comments are acceptable.

**5.34** When auditors receive written comments from the responsible officials, they should include in their report a copy of the officials' written comments, or a summary of the comments received. When the responsible officials provide oral comments only, auditors should prepare a summary of the oral comments and provide a copy of the summary to the responsible officials to verify that the comments are accurately stated.

---

[76]The steps taken will depend on the facts and circumstances, including legal considerations.

**5.35** Auditors should also include in the report an evaluation of the comments, as appropriate. In cases in which the audited entity provides technical comments in addition to its written or oral comments on the report, auditors may disclose in the report that such comments were received.

**5.36** Obtaining oral comments may be appropriate when, for example, there is a reporting date critical to meeting a user's needs; auditors have worked closely with the responsible officials throughout the conduct of the work and the parties are familiar with the findings and issues addressed in the draft report; or the auditors do not expect major disagreements with findings, conclusions, and recommendations in the draft report, or major controversies with regard to the issues discussed in the draft report.

**5.37** When the audited entity's comments are inconsistent or in conflict with findings, conclusions, or recommendations in the draft report, or when planned corrective actions do not adequately address the auditors' recommendations, the auditors should evaluate the validity of the audited entity's comments. If the auditors disagree with the comments, they should explain in the report their reasons for disagreement. Conversely, the auditors should modify their report as necessary if they find the comments valid and supported with sufficient, appropriate evidence.

**5.38** If the audited entity refuses to provide comments or is unable to provide comments within a reasonable period of time, the auditors may issue the report without receiving comments from the audited entity. In such cases, the auditors should indicate in the report that the audited entity did not provide comments.

## Reporting Confidential or Sensitive Information

**5.39** If certain pertinent information is prohibited from public disclosure or is excluded from a report due to the confidential or sensitive nature of the information, auditors should disclose in the report that certain information has been omitted and the reason or other circumstances that make the omission necessary.

**5.40** Certain information may be classified or may otherwise be prohibited from general disclosure by federal, state, or local laws or regulations. In such circumstances, auditors may issue a separate, classified, or limited use report containing the information and distribute the report only to persons authorized by law or regulation to receive it.

**5.41** Additional circumstances associated with public safety and security concerns could also justify the exclusion of certain information from a publicly available or widely distributed report. For example, detailed information related to computer security for a particular program may be excluded from publicly available reports because of the potential damage that could be caused by the misuse of this information. In such circumstances, auditors may issue a limited use report containing such information and distribute the report only to those parties responsible for acting on the auditors' recommendations. The auditors may consult with legal counsel regarding any requirements or other circumstances that may necessitate the omission of certain information.

**5.42** Considering the broad public interest in the program or activity under review assists auditors when deciding whether to exclude certain information from publicly available reports. When circumstances call for omission of certain information, auditors should evaluate whether this omission could distort the audit results or conceal improper or illegal practices.

**5.43** When audit organizations are subject to public records laws, auditors should determine whether public records laws could impact the availability of classified or limited use reports and determine whether other means of communicating with management and those charged with governance would be more appropriate. For example, the auditors may communicate general information in a written report and communicate detailed information verbally. The auditors may consult with legal counsel regarding applicable public records laws.

## Distributing Reports

**5.44** Distribution of reports completed under GAGAS depends on the relationship of the auditors to the audited organization and the nature of the information contained in the report. If the subject of the audit involves material that is classified for security purposes or contains confidential or sensitive information, auditors may limit the report distribution. Auditors should document any limitation on report distribution. The following discussion outlines distribution for reports completed under GAGAS:

**a.** Audit organizations in government entities should distribute audit reports to those charged with governance, to the appropriate officials of the audited entity, and to the appropriate oversight bodies or organizations requiring or arranging for the audits. As appropriate, auditors should also distribute copies of the reports to other officials who have legal oversight authority or who may be responsible for acting on audit findings and recommendations, and to others authorized to receive such reports.

**b.** Internal audit organizations in government entities may follow the Institute of Internal Auditors (IIA) *International Standards for the Professional Practice of Internal Auditing.* Under GAGAS and IIA standards, the head of the internal audit organization should communicate results to the parties who can ensure that the results are given due consideration. If not otherwise mandated by statutory or regulatory requirements, prior to releasing results to parties outside the organization, the head of the internal audit organization should: (1) assess the potential risk to the organization, (2) consult with senior management and/or legal counsel as appropriate, and (3) control dissemination by indicating the intended users in the report.

**c.** Public accounting firms contracted to perform an audit under GAGAS should clarify report distribution responsibilities with the engaging organization. If the contracted firm is to make the distribution, it should reach agreement with the party contracting for the audit about which officials or organizations will receive the report and the steps being taken to make the report available to the public.

# Chapter 6

# General, Field Work, and Reporting Standards for Attestation Engagements

| | |
|---|---|
| **Introduction** | **6.01** This chapter establishes standards and provides guidance for attestation engagements conducted in accordance with generally accepted government auditing standards (GAGAS). For attestation engagements, GAGAS incorporate the American Institute of Certified Public Accountants (AICPA) general standard on criteria, and the field work and reporting standards and the related Statements on Standards for Attestation Engagements (SSAE), unless specifically excluded or modified by GAGAS.[77],[78] This chapter identifies the AICPA general standard on criteria[79] and the field work and reporting standards for attestation engagements and prescribes additional standards for attestation engagements performed in accordance with GAGAS. |
| | **6.02** For attestation engagements performed in accordance with GAGAS, chapters 1 through 3 and 6 apply. |
| **AICPA General and Field Work Standards for Attestation Engagements** | **6.03** The AICPA general standard related to criteria is as follows: |
| | The practitioner [auditor] must have reason to believe that the subject matter is capable of evaluation against criteria that are suitable and available to users. |
| | **6.04** The two AICPA field work standards for attestation engagements are as follows: |

---

[77]To date, the Comptroller General has not excluded any field work standards, reporting standards, or SSAE.

[78]See AT Section 50, *SSAE Hierarchy.*

[79]GAGAS incorporate only one of the AICPA general standards for attestation engagements.

**a.** The practitioner [auditor] must adequately plan the work and must properly supervise any assistants.

**b.** The practitioner [auditor] must obtain sufficient evidence to provide a reasonable basis for the conclusion that is expressed in the report.

## Additional Government Auditing Standards

**6.05** GAGAS establish attestation engagement field work standards in addition to the requirements contained in the AICPA standards. Auditors should comply with these additional standards when citing GAGAS in their attestation engagement reports. The additional government auditing standards relate to

**a.** auditor communication during planning (see paragraphs 6.06 through 6.08);

**b.** previous audits and attestation engagements (see paragraph 6.09);

**c.** internal control (see paragraphs 6.10 through 6.12);

**d.** fraud, illegal acts, violations of provisions of contracts or grant agreements, or abuse that could have a material effect on the subject matter (see paragraphs 6.13 and 6.14);

**e.** developing elements of a finding (see paragraphs 6.15 through 6.19); and

**f.** documentation (see paragraphs 6.20 through 6.26).

## Auditor Communication During Planning

**6.06** Under AICPA standards and GAGAS, auditors should establish an understanding with the entity regarding the services to be performed for each engagement. Auditors also should obtain written acknowledgment or other evidence of the entity's responsibilities for the subject matter or the written assertion as it relates to the objectives of the engagement. GAGAS broaden the parties included in the communications during planning and contain additional items in the communications.

**6.07** Under GAGAS, when planning the engagement, auditors should communicate certain information, including their understanding of the services to be performed for each engagement, in writing to entity management, those charged with governance,[80] and to the individuals contracting for or requesting the engagement. When auditors perform the engagement pursuant to a law or regulation or they conduct the work for the legislative committee that has oversight of the entity, auditors should communicate with the legislative committee. In those situations where there is not a single individual or group that both oversees the strategic direction of the entity and the fulfillment of its accountability obligations or in other situations where the identity of those charged with governance is not clearly evident, the auditors should document the process followed and conclusions reached for identifying the appropriate individuals to receive the required auditor communications. Auditors should communicate the following additional information under GAGAS:

**a**. the nature, timing, and extent of planned testing and reporting;

**b**. the level of assurance the auditor will provide; and

---

[80]Those charged with governance are those responsible for overseeing the strategic direction of the entity and the entity's fulfillment of its obligations related to accountability. (See appendix I, paragraph A1.05 through A1.07 for additional information.)

**c.** any potential restriction on the auditors' reports, in order to reduce the risk that the needs or expectations of the parties involved may be misinterpreted.

**6.08** If an engagement is terminated before it is completed and a report is not issued, auditors should document the results of the work to the date of termination and why the engagement was terminated. Determining whether and how to communicate the reason for terminating the engagement to those charged with governance, appropriate officials of the entity, the entity contracting for or requesting the engagement, and other appropriate officials will depend on the facts and circumstances and, therefore, is a matter of professional judgment.

## Previous Audits and Attestation Engagements

**6.09** Auditors should evaluate whether the audited entity has taken appropriate corrective action to address findings and recommendations from previous engagements that could have a material effect on the subject matter. When planning the engagement, auditors should ask entity management to identify previous audits, attestation engagements, and other studies that directly relate to the subject matter of the attestation engagement being undertaken, including whether related recommendations have been implemented. Auditors should use this information in assessing risk and determining the nature, timing, and extent of current work, including determining the extent to which testing the implementation of the corrective actions is applicable to the current engagement objectives.

## Internal Control

**6.10** In planning examination-level attestation engagements, auditors should obtain a sufficient understanding of internal control that is material to the subject matter in order to plan the engagement and design procedures to achieve the objectives of the attestation engagement.

**6.11** In planning an examination-level attestation engagement, auditors should obtain an understanding of internal control as it relates to the subject matter to which the auditors are attesting. The subject matter may be financial or nonfinancial. (See paragraph 1.23 for a discussion of possible attestation engagement subject matters.)

**6.12** A deficiency in internal control exists when the design or operation of a control does not allow management or employees, in the normal course of performing their assigned functions, to prevent, detect, or correct errors in assertions made by management on a timely basis. A deficiency in design exists when (1) a control necessary to meet the control objective is missing or (2) an existing control is not properly designed so that, even if the control operates as designed, the control objective is not met. A deficiency in operation exists when a properly designed control does not operate as designed, or when the person performing the control does not possess the necessary authority or qualifications to perform the control effectively.

## Fraud, Illegal Acts, Violations of Provisions of Contracts or Grant Agreements, or Abuse That Could Have a Material Effect on the Subject Matter

**6.13** The auditors' responsibility with regard to fraud,[81] illegal acts, violations of provisions of contracts or grant agreements, or abuse for attestation engagements performed in accordance with GAGAS is as follows:

**a.** Examination-level engagements: In planning, auditors should design the engagement to provide reasonable assurance of detecting fraud, illegal acts, or violations of provisions of contracts or grant agreements that could have a material effect on the subject matter of the attestation engagement. Thus, auditors should assess the risk and possible effects of material fraud, illegal acts, or violations of provisions of contracts or grant agreements on the subject matter of the attestation engagement. When risk factors are identified, auditors should document the risk factors identified, the auditors' response to those risk factors individually or in combination, and the auditors' conclusions.

**b.** Review-level and agreed-upon-procedures-level engagements: If during the course of the engagement, information comes to the auditors' attention indicating that fraud, illegal acts, or violations of provisions of contracts or grant agreements that could have a material effect on the subject matter may have occurred, auditors should perform procedures as necessary to (1) determine if fraud, illegal acts, or violations of provisions of contracts or grant agreements are likely to have occurred and, if so, (2) determine their effect on the results of the attestation engagement. Auditors are not expected to provide assurance of detecting potential fraud, illegal acts, or violations of provisions of

---

[81]Fraud is a type of illegal act involving the obtaining of something of value through willful misrepresentation. Although not applicable to attestation engagements, the AICPA Statements on Auditing Standards (SAS) may provide useful guidance related to fraud for auditors performing attestation engagements in accordance with GAGAS.

contracts or grant agreements for these types of engagements unless it is specified in the procedures.

**c.** For all levels of attestation engagements: If during the course of the engagement, auditors become aware of abuse that could be quantitatively or qualitatively material, auditors should apply procedures specifically directed to ascertain the potential effect on the subject matter or other data significant to the engagement objectives. After performing additional work, auditors may discover that the abuse represents potential fraud or illegal acts. Because the determination of abuse is subjective, auditors are not required to provide reasonable assurance of detecting abuse in attestation engagements.

**6.14** Abuse involves behavior that is deficient or improper when compared with behavior that a prudent person would consider reasonable and necessary business practice given the facts and circumstances. Abuse also includes misuse of authority or position for personal financial interests or those of an immediate or close family member or business associate. Abuse does not necessarily involve fraud, violation of laws, regulations, or provisions of a contract or grant agreement.

## Developing Elements of a Finding

**6.15** Audit findings may involve deficiencies in internal control, fraud, illegal acts, violations of provisions of contracts or grant agreements, and abuse. The elements needed for a finding depend entirely on the engagement objectives. Thus a finding or set of findings is complete to the extent that the engagement objectives are satisfied. When auditors identify deficiencies, auditors should plan and perform procedures to develop the elements of the findings that are relevant and necessary to achieve the engagement objectives. The elements of a finding are discussed in paragraphs 6.16 through 6.19.

**6.16** Criteria: The laws, regulations, contracts, grant agreements, standards, measures, expected performance, defined business practices, and benchmarks against which performance is compared or evaluated. Criteria identify the required or desired state or expectation with respect to the program or operation. Criteria provide a context for evaluating evidence and understanding the findings.

**6.17** Condition: Condition is a situation that exists. The condition is determined and documented during the engagement.

**6.18** Cause: The cause identifies the reason or explanation for the condition or the factor or factors responsible for the difference between the situation that exists (condition) and the required or desired state (criteria), which may also serve as a basis for recommendations for corrective actions. Common factors include poorly designed policies, procedures, or criteria; inconsistent, incomplete, or incorrect implementation; or factors beyond the control of program management. Auditors may assess whether the evidence provides a reasonable and convincing argument for why the stated cause is the key factor or factors contributing to the difference.

**6.19** Effect or potential effect: The effect is a clear, logical link to establish the impact or potential impact of the difference between the situation that exists (condition) and the required or desired state (criteria). The effect or potential effect identifies the outcomes or consequences of the condition. When the engagement objectives include identifying the actual or potential consequences of a condition that varies (either positively or negatively) from the criteria identified in the engagement, "effect" is a measure of those consequences. Effect or potential effect may be used to demonstrate the need for corrective action in response to identified problems or relevant risks.

## Attest Documentation

**6.20** Under GAGAS, auditors must prepare attest documentation in connection with each engagement in sufficient detail to provide a clear understanding of the work performed (including the nature, timing, extent, and results of engagement procedures performed); the evidence obtained and its source; and the conclusions reached. Documentation provides the principal support for

**a.** the statement in the engagement report that the auditors performed the attestation engagement in accordance with GAGAS and any other standards cited and

**b.** the auditors' conclusion.

**6.21** Auditors should prepare attest documentation in sufficient detail to enable an experienced auditor,[82] having no previous connection to the attestation engagement, to understand from the documentation the nature, timing, extent, and results of procedures performed and the evidence obtained and its source and the conclusions reached, including evidence that supports the auditors' significant judgments and conclusions. Auditors should prepare attest documentation that contains support for findings,

---

[82]An experienced auditor means an individual (whether internal or external to the audit organization) who possesses the competencies and skills that would have enabled him or her to perform the attestation engagement. These competencies and skills include an understanding of (1) attestation engagement processes, (2) GAGAS and applicable legal and regulatory requirements, (3) the subject matter that the auditor is engaged to report on, (4) the suitability and availability of criteria, and (5) issues related to the audited entity's environment.

conclusions, and recommendations before they issue their report.

**6.22** Auditors also should document the following for attestation engagements performed under GAGAS:

**a.** the objectives, scope, and methodology of the attestation engagement;

**b.** the work performed to support significant judgments and conclusions, including descriptions of transactions and records examined;[83]

**c.** evidence of supervisory review, before the engagement report is issued, of the work performed that supports findings, conclusions, and recommendations contained in the engagement report; and

**d.** the auditors' consideration that the planned procedures be designed to achieve objectives of the attestation engagement when (1) evidence obtained is dependent on computerized information systems, (2) such evidence is material to the objective of the engagement, and (3) the auditors are not relying on the effectiveness of internal control over those computerized systems that produced the evidence. Auditors should document (1) the rationale for determining the nature, timing, and extent of planned procedures; (2) the kinds and competence of available evidence produced outside a computerized information system, or plans for direct testing of data produced from a computerized information system; and (3) the effect on the attestation engagement report if evidence to be

---

[83]Auditors may meet this requirement by listing file numbers, case numbers, or other means of identifying specific documents they examined. They are not required to include copies of documents they examined as part of the attest documentation, nor are they required to list detailed information from those documents.

gathered does not afford a reasonable basis for
achieving the objectives of the engagement.

**6.23** When auditors do not comply with applicable
GAGAS requirements due to law, regulation, scope
limitations, restrictions on access to records, or other
issues impacting the engagement, the auditors should
document the departure, the impact on the engagement
and on the auditors' conclusions. This applies to
departures from mandatory requirements and
presumptively mandatory requirements where
alternative procedures performed in the circumstances
were not sufficient to achieve the objectives of the
standard. (See paragraphs 1.12 and 1.13.)

**6.24** Audit organizations should establish policies and
procedures for the safe custody and retention of
documentation for a time sufficient to satisfy legal,
regulatory, and administrative requirements for records
retention. Whether engagement documentation is in
paper, electronic, or other media, the integrity,
accessibility, and retrievability of the underlying
information could be compromised if the
documentation is altered, added to, or deleted without
the auditors' knowledge, or if the documentation is lost
or damaged. For attest documentation that is retained
electronically, the audit organization should establish
information systems controls concerning accessing and
updating the attest documentation.

**6.25** Underlying GAGAS engagements is the premise
that audit organizations in federal, state, and local
governments and public accounting firms engaged to
perform an engagement in accordance with GAGAS
cooperate in performing attestation engagements of
programs of common interest so that auditors may use
others' work and avoid duplication of efforts. Subject to
applicable laws and regulations, auditors should make
appropriate individuals, as well as attest documentation,

available upon request and in a timely manner to other auditors or reviewers to satisfy these objectives. The use of auditors' work by other auditors may be facilitated by contractual arrangements for GAGAS engagements that provide for full and timely access to appropriate individuals, as well as attest documentation.

**6.26** Audit organizations should develop policies to deal with requests by outside parties to obtain access to attest documentation, especially when an outside party attempts to obtain information indirectly through the auditor rather than directly from the entity. In developing such policies, audit organizations should determine what laws and regulations apply, if any.

## Additional Considerations for GAGAS Attestation Engagements

**6.27** Due to the engagement objectives and public accountability of GAGAS engagements, there may be additional considerations for attestation engagements completed in accordance with GAGAS. These considerations relate to

**a.** materiality in GAGAS attestation engagements (see paragraph 6.28) and

**b.** ongoing investigations or legal proceedings (see paragraph 6.29).

## Materiality in GAGAS Attestation Engagements

**6.28** The concept of materiality recognizes that some matters, either individually or in the aggregate, are important for fair presentation of a subject matter or an assertion about a subject matter, while other matters are not important. In performing the engagement, matters that, either individually or in the aggregate, could be material to the subject matter are a primary consideration. In engagements performed in accordance with GAGAS, auditors may find it appropriate to use lower materiality levels as compared with the materiality levels used in non-GAGAS engagements because of the public accountability of government entities and entities receiving government funding, various legal and regulatory requirements, and the visibility and sensitivity of government programs.

## Ongoing Investigations or Legal Proceedings

**6.29** Avoiding interference with investigations or legal proceedings is important in pursuing indications of fraud, illegal acts, violations of provisions of contracts or grant agreements, or abuse. Laws, regulations, or policies might require auditors to report indications of certain types of fraud, illegal acts, violations of provisions of contracts or grant agreements, or abuse to law enforcement or investigatory authorities before performing additional procedures. When investigations or legal proceedings are initiated or in process, auditors should evaluate the impact on the current engagement. In some cases, it may be appropriate for the auditors to work with investigators and/or legal authorities, or withdraw from or defer further work on the engagement or a portion of the engagement to avoid interfering with an investigation.

## AICPA Reporting Standards for Attestation Engagements

**6.30** The four AICPA reporting standards that apply to all levels of attestation engagements are as follows:[84]

**a.** The practitioner [auditor] must identify the subject matter or the assertion being reported on and state the character of the engagement in the report.

**b.** The practitioner [auditor] must state the practitioner's [auditor's] conclusion about the subject matter or the

---

[84]Under AT Section 50, *SSAE Hierarchy*, the reporting standards apply when the practitioner issues a report. The reporting standards do not apply when the practitioner declines to issue a report as a result of the engagement.

assertion in relation to the criteria against which the subject matter was evaluated in the report.

**c.** The practitioner [auditor] must state all of the practitioner's [auditor's] significant reservations about the engagement, the subject matter, and, if applicable, the assertion related thereto in the report.

**d.** The practitioner [auditor] must state in the report that the report is intended for use by specified parties under the following circumstances:

**(1)** When the criteria used to evaluate the subject matter are determined by the practitioner [auditor] to be appropriate only for a limited number of parties who either participated in their establishment or can be presumed to have an adequate understanding of the criteria.

**(2)** When the criteria used to evaluate the subject matter are available only to specified parties.

**(3)** When reporting on subject matter and a written assertion has not been provided by the responsible party.

**(4)** When the report is on an attest engagement to apply agreed-upon procedures to the subject matter.

## Additional Government Auditing Standards

**6.31** GAGAS establish reporting standards for attestation engagements in addition to the requirements contained in the AICPA standards. Auditors should comply with these additional standards when citing GAGAS in their attestation engagement reports. The additional government auditing standards relate to

**a.** reporting auditors' compliance with GAGAS (see paragraph 6.32);

**b.** reporting deficiencies in internal control, fraud, illegal acts, violations of provisions of contracts or grant agreements, and abuse (see paragraphs 6.33 through 6.43);

**c.** reporting views of responsible officials (see paragraphs 6.44 through 6.50);

**d.** reporting confidential or sensitive information (see paragraphs 6.51 through 6.55); and

**e.** distributing reports (see paragraph 6.56).

## Reporting Auditors' Compliance with GAGAS

**6.32** When auditors comply with all applicable GAGAS requirements, they should include a statement in the attestation report that they performed the engagement in accordance with GAGAS. (See paragraphs 1.12 and 1.13 for additional requirements on citing compliance with GAGAS.) GAGAS do not prohibit auditors from issuing a separate report conforming only to the requirements of other standards.

## Reporting Deficiencies in Internal Control, Fraud, Illegal Acts, Violations of Provisions of Contracts or Grant Agreements, and Abuse

**6.33** For attestation engagements, auditors should report, as applicable to the objectives of the engagement, and based upon the work performed, (1) significant deficiencies in internal control, identifying those considered to be material weaknesses; (2) all instances of fraud and illegal acts unless inconsequential; and (3) violations of provisions of contracts or grant agreements and abuse that could have a material effect on the subject matter of the engagement.

### Deficiencies in Internal Control

**6.34** For all attestation engagements, auditors should report the following deficiencies in internal control:

**a.** Significant deficiency: a deficiency in internal control, or combination of deficiencies, that adversely affects the entity's ability to initiate, authorize, record, process, or report data reliably in accordance with the applicable criteria or framework such that there is more than a remote[85] likelihood that a misstatement of the subject matter that is more than inconsequential[86] will not be prevented or detected.

**b.** Material weakness: a significant deficiency or combination of significant deficiencies, that results in more than a remote likelihood that a material misstatement of the subject matter will not be prevented or detected.

**6.35** Determining whether and how to communicate to entity officials internal control deficiencies that have an inconsequential effect on the subject matter is a matter of professional judgment. Auditors should document such communications.

**Fraud, Illegal Acts, Violations of Provisions of Contracts or Grant Agreements, and Abuse**

**6.36** Under GAGAS, when auditors conclude, based on sufficient, appropriate evidence, that any of the following either has occurred or is likely to have occurred, they should include in their report the relevant information about

---

[85]The term "more than remote" used in the definitions for significant deficiency and material weakness means "at least reasonably possible." The following definitions apply: (1) Remote—The chance of the future events occurring is slight. (2) Reasonably possible—The chance of the future events or their occurrence is more than remote but less than likely. (3) Probable—The future events are likely to occur.

[86]"More than inconsequential" indicates an amount that is less than material, yet has significance. A misstatement is "inconsequential" if a reasonable person would conclude that the misstatement, either individually or when aggregated with other misstatements, would clearly be immaterial to the subject matter. If a reasonable person would not reach such a conclusion, that misstatement is "more than inconsequential."

**a**. fraud and illegal acts[87] that have an effect on the subject matter that is more than inconsequential,

**b.** violations of provisions of contracts or grant agreements that have a material effect on the subject matter, and

**c.** abuse that is material to the subject matter, either quantitatively or qualitatively. (See paragraphs 6.13 and 6.14 for a discussion of abuse.)

**6.37** When auditors detect violations of provisions of contracts or grant agreements or abuse that have an effect on the subject matter that is less than material but more than inconsequential, they should communicate those findings in writing to entity officials. Determining whether and how to communicate to entity officials fraud, illegal acts, violations of provisions of contracts or grant agreements, or abuse that is inconsequential is a matter of professional judgment. Auditors should document such communications.

**6.38** When fraud, illegal acts, violations of provisions of contracts or grant agreements, or abuse either have occurred or are likely to have occurred, auditors may consult with authorities or legal counsel about whether publicly reporting such information would compromise investigative or legal proceedings. Auditors may limit their public reporting to matters that would not compromise those proceedings and, for example, report only on information that is already a part of the public record.

---

[87]Whether a particular act is, in fact, illegal may have to await final determination by a court of law or other adjudicative body. Disclosing matters that have led auditors to conclude that an illegal act is likely to have occurred is not a final determination of illegality.

Reporting Findings
Directly to Parties
Outside the Entity

**6.39** Auditors should report known or likely fraud, illegal acts, violations of provisions of contracts or grant agreements, or abuse directly to parties outside the audited entity in the following two circumstances.[88]

**a.** When entity management fails to satisfy legal or regulatory requirements to report such information to external parties specified in law or regulation, auditors should first communicate the failure to report such information to those charged with governance. If the audited entity still does not report this information to the specified external parties as soon as practicable after the auditors' communication with those charged with governance, then the auditors should report the information directly to the specified external parties.

**b.** When entity management fails to take timely and appropriate steps to respond to known or likely fraud, illegal acts, violations of provisions of contracts or grant agreements, or abuse that (1) is likely to have a material effect on the subject matter and (2) involves funding received directly or indirectly from a government agency, auditors should first report management's failure to take timely and appropriate steps to those charged with governance. If the audited entity still does not take timely and appropriate steps as soon as practicable after the auditors' communication with those charged with governance, then the auditors should report the entity's failure to take timely and appropriate steps directly to the funding agency.

**6.40** The reporting in paragraph 6.39 is in addition to any legal requirements to report such information directly to parties outside the entity. Auditors should

---

[88]Internal audit organizations do not have a duty to report outside the entity unless required by law, rule, regulation, or policy. (See paragraph 6.56b for reporting standards for internal audit organizations when reporting externally.)

comply with these requirements even if they have resigned or been dismissed from the engagement prior to its completion.

**6.41** Auditors should obtain sufficient, appropriate evidence, such as confirmation from outside parties, to corroborate assertions by entity management that it has reported such findings in accordance with laws, regulations, and funding agreements. When auditors are unable to do so, they should report such information directly as discussed in paragraph 6.39.

**Presenting Findings in the Auditors' Report**

**6.42** In presenting findings such as deficiencies in internal control, fraud, illegal acts, violations of provisions of contracts or grant agreements, and abuse, auditors should develop the elements of the findings to the extent necessary to achieve the engagement objectives. Clearly developed findings, as discussed in paragraphs 6.15 through 6.19, assist management or oversight officials in understanding the need for taking corrective action. If auditors are able to sufficiently develop the elements of a finding, they may provide recommendations for corrective action.

**6.43** Auditors should place their findings in perspective by describing the nature and extent of the issues being reported and the extent of the work performed that resulted in the finding. To give the reader a basis for judging the prevalence and consequences of these findings, auditors should, as applicable, relate the instances identified to the population or the number of cases examined and quantify the results in terms of dollar value or other measures, as appropriate. If the results cannot be projected, auditors should limit their conclusions appropriately.

**Reporting Views of Responsible Officials**

**6.44** If the attestation engagement report discloses deficiencies in internal control, fraud, illegal acts,

violations of provisions of contracts or grant
agreements, or abuse, auditors should obtain and report
the views of responsible officials concerning the
findings, conclusions, and recommendations, as well as
planned corrective actions.

**6.45** Providing a draft report with findings for review
and comment by responsible officials of the audited
entity and others helps the auditors develop a report
that is fair, complete, and objective. Including the views
of responsible officials results in a report that presents
not only the auditors' findings, conclusions, and
recommendations, but also the perspectives of the
responsible officials of the audited entity and the
corrective actions they plan to take. Obtaining the
comments in writing is preferred, but oral comments are
acceptable.

**6.46** When auditors receive written comments from the
responsible officials, they should include in their report
a copy of the officials' written comments, or a summary
of the comments received. When the responsible
officials provide oral comments only, auditors should
prepare a summary of the oral comments and provide a
copy of the summary to the responsible officials to
verify that the comments are accurately stated.

**6.47** Auditors should also include in the report an
evaluation of the comments, as appropriate. In cases in
which the audited entity provides technical comments in
addition to its written or oral comments on the report,
auditors may disclose in the report that such comments
were received.

**6.48** Obtaining oral comments may be appropriate
when, for example, there is a reporting date critical to
meeting a user's needs; auditors have worked closely
with the responsible officials throughout the conduct of
the work and the parties are familiar with the findings

and issues addressed in the draft report; or the auditors do not expect major disagreements with the findings, conclusions, and recommendations in the draft report, or major controversies with regard to the issues discussed in the draft report.

**6.49** When the entity's comments are inconsistent or in conflict with the findings, conclusions, or recommendations in the draft report, or when planned corrective actions do not adequately address the auditors' recommendations, the auditors should evaluate the validity of the audited entity's comments. If the auditors disagree with the comments, they should explain in the report their reasons for disagreement. Conversely, the auditors should modify their report as necessary if they find the comments valid and supported with sufficient, appropriate evidence.

**6.50** If the entity refuses to provide comments or is unable to provide comments within a reasonable period of time, the auditors may issue the report without receiving comments from the entity. In such cases, the auditors should indicate in the report that the audited entity did not provide comments.

## Reporting Confidential or Sensitive Information

**6.51** If certain pertinent information is prohibited from public disclosure or is excluded from a report due to the confidential or sensitive nature of the information, auditors should disclose in the report that certain information has been omitted and the reason or other circumstances that make the omission necessary.

**6.52** Certain information may be classified or may be otherwise prohibited from general disclosure by federal, state, or local laws or regulations. In such circumstances, auditors may issue a separate classified or limited use report containing such information and distribute the report only to persons authorized by law or regulation to receive it.

**6.53** Additional circumstances associated with public safety and security concerns could also justify the exclusion of certain information from a publicly available or widely distributed report. For example, detailed information related to computer security for a particular program may be excluded from publicly available reports because of the potential damage that could be caused by the misuse of this information. In such circumstances, auditors may issue a limited use report containing such information and distribute the report only to those parties responsible for acting on the auditors' recommendations. The auditors may consult with legal counsel regarding any requirements or other circumstances that may necessitate the omission of certain information.

**6.54** Considering the broad public interest in the program or activity under review assists auditors when deciding whether to exclude certain information from publicly available reports. When circumstances call for omission of certain information, auditors should evaluate whether this omission could distort the engagement results or conceal improper or illegal practices.

**6.55** When audit organizations are subject to public records laws, auditors should determine whether public records laws could impact the availability of classified or limited use reports and determine whether other means of communicating with management and those charged with governance would be more appropriate. For example, the auditors may communicate general information in a written report and communicate detailed information verbally. The auditor may consult with legal counsel regarding applicable public records laws.

Distributing Reports

**6.56** Distribution of reports completed under GAGAS depends on the relationship of the auditors to the entity and the nature of the information contained in the report. If the subject matter or the assertion involves material that is classified for security purposes or contains confidential or sensitive information, auditors may limit the report distribution. Auditors should document any limitation on report distribution. The following discussion outlines distribution for reports completed under GAGAS:

**a.** Audit organizations in government entities should distribute reports to those charged with governance, to the appropriate entity officials, and to the appropriate oversight bodies or organizations requiring or arranging for the engagements. As appropriate, auditors should also distribute copies of the reports to other officials who have legal oversight authority or who may be responsible for acting on engagement findings and recommendations, and to others authorized to receive such reports.

**b.** Internal audit organizations in government entities may follow the Institute of Internal Auditors (IIA) *International Standards for the Professional Practice of Internal Auditing.* Under GAGAS and IIA standards, the head of the internal audit organization should communicate results to the parties who can ensure that the results are given due consideration. If not otherwise mandated by statutory or regulatory requirements, prior to releasing results to parties outside the organization, the head of the internal audit organization should: (1) assess the potential risk to the organization, (2) consult with senior management and/or legal counsel as appropriate, and (3) control dissemination by indicating the intended users in the report.

**c.** Public accounting firms contracted to perform an engagement under GAGAS should clarify report distribution responsibilities with the engaging organization. If the contracting firm is to make the distribution, it should reach agreement with the party contracting for the engagement about which officials or organizations will receive the report and the steps being taken to make the report available to the public.

# Chapter 7

# Field Work Standards for Performance Audits

Introduction

**7.01** This chapter establishes field work standards and provides guidance for performance audits conducted in accordance with generally accepted government auditing standards (GAGAS). The field work standards for performance audits relate to planning the audit; supervising staff; obtaining sufficient, appropriate evidence; and preparing audit documentation. The concepts of reasonable assurance, significance, and audit risk form a framework for applying these standards and are included throughout the discussion of performance audits.

**7.02** For performance audits performed in accordance with GAGAS, chapters 1 through 3 and 7 and 8 apply.

Reasonable Assurance

**7.03** Performance audits that comply with GAGAS provide reasonable assurance that evidence is sufficient and appropriate to support the auditors' findings and conclusions. Thus, the sufficiency and appropriateness of evidence needed and tests of evidence will vary based on the audit objectives, findings, and conclusions. Objectives for performance audits range from narrow to broad and involve varying types and quality of evidence. In some engagements, sufficient, appropriate evidence is available, but in others, information may have limitations. Professional judgment assists auditors in determining the audit scope and methodology needed to address the audit objectives, while providing the appropriate level of assurance that the obtained evidence is sufficient and appropriate to address the audit objectives. (See paragraphs 7.55 through 7.71 for a discussion about assessing the sufficiency and appropriateness of evidence.)

## Significance in a Performance Audit

**7.04** The concept of significance[89] assists auditors throughout a performance audit, including when deciding the type and extent of audit work to perform, when evaluating results of audit work, and when developing the report and related findings and conclusions. Significance is defined as the relative importance of a matter within the context in which it is being considered, including quantitative and qualitative factors. Such factors include the magnitude of the matter in relation to the subject matter of the audit, the nature and effect of the matter, the relevance of the matter, the needs and interests of an objective third party with knowledge of the relevant information, and the impact of the matter to the audited program or activity. Professional judgment assists auditors when evaluating the significance of matters within the context of the audit objectives.

## Audit Risk

**7.05** Audit risk is the possibility that the auditors' findings, conclusions, recommendations, or assurance may be improper or incomplete, as a result of factors such as evidence that is not sufficient and/or appropriate, an inadequate audit process, or intentional omissions or misleading information due to misrepresentation or fraud. The assessment of audit risk involves both qualitative and quantitative considerations. Factors such as the time frames, complexity, or sensitivity of the work; size of the program in terms of dollar amounts and number of citizens served; adequacy of the audited entity's systems and processes to detect inconsistencies, significant errors, or fraud; and auditors' access to records, also impact audit risk. Audit risk includes the risk that

---

[89]In the performance audit standards, the term "significant" is comparable to the term "material" as used in the context of financial statement audits.

auditors will not detect a mistake, inconsistency, significant error, or fraud in the evidence supporting the audit. Audit risk can be reduced by taking actions such as increasing the scope of work; adding experts, additional reviewers, and other resources to the audit team; changing the methodology to obtain additional evidence, higher quality evidence, or alternative forms of corroborating evidence; or aligning the findings and conclusions to reflect the evidence obtained.

## Planning

**7.06** Auditors must adequately plan and document the planning of the work necessary to address the audit objectives.

**7.07** Auditors must plan the audit to reduce audit risk to an appropriate level for the auditors to provide reasonable assurance that the evidence is sufficient and appropriate to support the auditors' findings and conclusions. This determination is a matter of professional judgment. In planning the audit, auditors should assess significance and audit risk and apply these assessments in defining the audit objectives and the scope and methodology to address those objectives.[90] Planning is a continuous process throughout the audit. Therefore, auditors may need to adjust the audit objectives, scope, and methodology as work is being completed.

**7.08** The objectives are what the audit is intended to accomplish. They identify the audit subject matter and performance aspects to be included, and may also include the potential findings and reporting elements that the auditors expect to develop. Audit objectives can

---

[90]In situations where the audit objectives are established by statute or legislative oversight, auditors may not have latitude to define the audit objectives or scope.

be thought of as questions about the program[91] that the auditors seek to answer based on evidence obtained and assessed against criteria.

**7.09** Scope is the boundary of the audit and is directly tied to the audit objectives. The scope defines the subject matter that the auditors will assess and report on, such as a particular program or aspect of a program, the necessary documents or records, the period of time reviewed, and the locations that will be included.

**7.10** The methodology describes the nature and extent of audit procedures for gathering and analyzing evidence to address the audit objectives. Audit procedures are the specific steps and tests auditors will carry out to address the audit objectives. Auditors should design the methodology to obtain sufficient, appropriate evidence to address the audit objectives, reduce audit risk to an acceptable level, and provide reasonable assurance that the evidence is sufficient and appropriate to support the auditors' findings and conclusions. Methodology includes both the nature and extent of audit procedures used to address the audit objectives.

 **7.11** Auditors should assess audit risk and significance within the context of the audit objectives by gaining an understanding of the following:

**a.** the nature and profile of the programs and the needs of potential users of the audit report (see paragraphs 7.13 through 7.15);

---

[91]The term "program" is used in this document to include government entities, organizations, programs, activities, and functions.

**b.** internal control as it relates to the specific objectives and scope of the audit (see paragraphs 7.16 through 7.22);

**c.** information systems controls for purposes of assessing audit risk and planning the audit within the context of the audit objectives (see paragraphs 7.23 through 7.27);

**d.** legal and regulatory requirements, contract provisions or grant agreements, potential fraud, or abuse that are significant within the context of the audit objectives (see paragraphs 7.28 through 7.35); and

**e.** the results of previous audits and attestation engagements that directly relate to the current audit objectives (see paragraph 7.36).

**7.12** During planning, auditors also should

**a.** identify the potential criteria needed to evaluate matters subject to audit (see paragraphs 7.37 and 7.38);

**b.** identify sources of audit evidence and determine the amount and type of evidence needed given audit risk and significance (see paragraphs 7.39 and 7.40);

**c.** evaluate whether to use the work of other auditors and experts to address some of the audit objectives (see paragraphs 7.41 through 7.43);

**d.** assign sufficient staff and specialists with adequate collective professional competence and identify other resources needed to perform the audit (see paragraphs 7.44 and 7.45);

**e.** communicate about planning and performance of the audit to management officials, those charged with governance, and others as applicable (see paragraphs 7.46 through 7.49); and

**f.** prepare a written audit plan (see paragraphs 7.50 and 7.51).

## Nature and Profile of the Program and User Needs

**7.13** Auditors should obtain an understanding of the nature of the program or program component under audit and the potential use that will be made of the audit results or report as they plan a performance audit. The nature and profile of a program include

**a.** visibility, sensitivity, and relevant risks associated with the program under audit;

**b.** age of the program or changes in its conditions;

**c.** the size of the program in terms of total dollars, number of citizens affected, or other measures;

**d.** level and extent of review or other forms of independent oversight;

**e.** program's strategic plan and objectives; and

**f.** external factors or conditions that could directly affect the program.

**7.14** One group of users of the auditors' report is government officials who may have authorized or requested the audit. Other important users of the auditors' report are the entity being audited, those responsible for acting on the auditors' recommendations, oversight organizations, and legislative bodies. Other potential users of the auditors' report include government legislators or officials (other than those who may have authorized or requested the audit), the media, interest groups, and individual citizens. In addition to an interest in the program, potential users may have an ability to influence the conduct of the program. An awareness of these potential users' interests and influence can help auditors judge whether possible findings could be significant to relevant users.

**7.15** Obtaining an understanding of the program under audit helps auditors to assess the relevant risks associated with the program and the impact on the audit objectives, scope, and methodology. The auditors' understanding may come from knowledge they already have about the program or knowledge they gain from inquiries and observations they make in planning the audit. The extent and breadth of those inquiries and observations will vary among audits based on the audit objectives, as will the need to understand individual aspects of the program, such as the following.

**a.** Laws, regulations, and provisions of contracts or grant agreements: Government programs are usually created by law and are subject to specific laws and regulations. Laws and regulations usually set forth what is to be done, who is to do it, the purpose to be achieved, the population to be served, and related funding guidelines or restrictions. Government programs may also be subject to provisions of contracts and grant agreements. Thus, understanding the laws and legislative history establishing a program and the provisions of any contracts or grant agreements can be essential to understanding the program itself. Obtaining that understanding is also a necessary step in identifying the provisions of laws, regulations, contracts, or grant agreements that are significant within the context of the audit objectives.

**b.** Purpose and goals: Purpose is the result or effect that is intended or desired from a program's operation. Legislatures usually establish the program's purpose when they provide authority for the program. Entity officials may provide more detailed information on the program's purpose to supplement the authorizing legislation. Entity officials are sometimes asked to set goals for program performance and operations, including both output and outcome goals. Auditors may use the stated program purpose and goals as criteria for assessing program performance or may develop additional criteria to use when assessing performance.

c. Internal control: Internal control, sometimes referred to as management control, in the broadest sense includes the plan, policies, methods, and procedures adopted by management to meet its missions, goals, and objectives. Internal control includes the processes for planning, organizing, directing, and controlling program operations. It includes the systems for measuring, reporting, and monitoring program performance. Internal control serves as a defense in safeguarding assets and in preventing and detecting errors; fraud; violations of laws, regulations, and provisions of contracts and grant agreements; or abuse. Paragraphs 7.16 through 7.22 contain guidance pertaining to internal control.

d. Efforts: Efforts are the amount of resources (in terms of money, material, personnel, etc.) that are put into a program. These resources may come from within or outside the entity operating the program. Measures of efforts can have a number of dimensions, such as cost, timing, and quality. Examples of measures of efforts are dollars spent, employee-hours expended, and square feet of building space.

e. Program operations: Program operations are the strategies, processes, and activities management uses to convert efforts into outputs. Program operations may be subject to internal control.

**f.** Outputs: Outputs represent the quantity of goods or services produced by a program. For example, an output measure for a job training program could be the number of persons completing training, and an output measure for an aviation safety inspection program could be the number of safety inspections completed.

**g.** Outcomes: Outcomes are accomplishments or results of a program. For example, an outcome measure for a job training program could be the percentage of trained persons obtaining a job and still in the work place after a specified period of time. An example of an outcome measure for an aviation safety inspection program could be the percentage reduction in safety problems found in subsequent inspections or the percentage of problems deemed corrected in follow-up inspections. Such outcome measures show the progress made in achieving the stated program purpose of helping unemployable citizens obtain and retain jobs, and improving the safety of aviation operations. Outcomes may be influenced by cultural, economic, physical, or technological factors outside the program. Auditors may use approaches drawn from other disciplines, such as program evaluation, to isolate the effects of the program from these other influences. Outcomes also include unexpected and/or unintentional effects of a program, both positive and negative.

Internal Control

*Review*

**7.16** Auditors should obtain an understanding of internal control[92] that is significant within the context of the audit objectives. For internal control that is significant within the context of the audit objectives, auditors should assess whether internal control has been properly designed and implemented. For those internal controls that are deemed significant within the context of the audit objectives, auditors should plan to obtain sufficient, appropriate evidence to support their assessment about the effectiveness of those controls. Information systems controls are often an integral part of an entity's internal control. Thus, when obtaining an understanding of internal control significant to the audit objectives, auditors should also determine whether it is necessary to evaluate information systems controls. (See paragraphs 7.23 through 7.27 for additional discussion on evaluating the effectiveness of information systems controls.)

**7.17** Auditors may modify the nature, timing, or extent of the audit procedures based on the auditors' assessment of internal control and the results of internal

---

[92]Refer to the internal control guidance contained in *Internal Control--Integrated Framework*, published by the Committee of Sponsoring Organizations of the Treadway Commission (COSO). As discussed in the COSO framework, internal control consists of five interrelated components, which are (1) control environment, (2) risk assessment, (3) control activities, (4) information and communication, and (5) monitoring. The objectives of internal control relate to (1) financial reporting, (2) operations, and (3) compliance. Safeguarding of assets is a subset of these objectives. In that respect, management designs internal control to provide reasonable assurance that unauthorized acquisition, use, or disposition of assets will be prevented or timely detected and corrected. In addition to the COSO document, the publication, *Standards for Internal Control in the Federal Government*, GAO/AIMD-00-21.3.1 (Washington, D.C.: November 1999), which incorporates the relevant guidance developed by COSO, provides definitions and fundamental concepts pertaining to internal control at the federal level and may be useful to other auditors at any level of government. The related *Internal Control Management and Evaluation Tool*, GAO-01-1008G (Washington, D.C.: August 2001), based on the federal internal control standards, provides a systematic, organized, and structured approach to assessing the internal control structure.

control testing. For example, poorly controlled aspects of a program have a higher risk of failure, so auditors may choose to focus their efforts in these areas. Conversely, effective controls at the audited entity may enable the auditors to limit the extent and type of audit testing needed.

**7.18** Auditors may obtain an understanding of internal control through inquiries, observations, inspection of documents and records, review of other auditors' reports, or direct tests. The procedures auditors perform to obtain an understanding of internal control may vary among audits based on audit objectives and audit risk. The extent of these procedures will vary based on the audit objectives, known or potential internal control risks or problems, and the auditors' knowledge about internal control gained in prior audits.

**7.19** The following discussion of the principal types of internal control objectives is intended to help auditors better understand internal controls and determine whether or to what extent they are significant to the audit objectives.

**a.** Effectiveness and efficiency of program operations: Controls over program operations include policies and procedures that the audited entity has implemented to provide reasonable assurance that a program meets its objectives, while considering cost-effectiveness and efficiency. Understanding these controls can help auditors understand the program operations that convert inputs and efforts to outputs and outcomes.

**b.** Relevance and reliability of information: Controls over the relevance and reliability of information include policies, procedures, and practices that officials of the audited entity have implemented to provide themselves reasonable assurance that operational and financial information they use for decision making and reporting externally is relevant and reliable and fairly disclosed in reports. Understanding these controls can help auditors (1) assess the risk that the information gathered by the entity may not be relevant or reliable and (2) design appropriate tests of the information considering the audit objectives.

**c.** Compliance with applicable laws and regulations and provisions of contracts or grant agreements: Controls over compliance include policies and procedures that the audited entity has implemented to provide reasonable assurance that program implementation is in accordance with laws, regulations, and provisions of contracts or grant agreements. Understanding the relevant controls concerning compliance with those laws and regulations and provisions of contracts or grant agreements that the auditors have determined are significant within the context of the audit objectives can help them assess the risk of illegal acts, violations of provisions of contracts or grant agreements, or abuse.

**7.20** A subset of these categories of internal control objectives is the safeguarding of assets and resources. Controls over the safeguarding of assets and resources include policies and procedures that the audited entity has implemented to reasonably prevent or promptly detect unauthorized acquisition, use, or disposition of assets and resources.

**7.21** In performance audits, a deficiency in internal control exists when the design or operation of a control does not allow management or employees, in the normal course of performing their assigned functions, to prevent, detect, or correct (1) impairments of effectiveness or efficiency of operations, (2) misstatements in financial or performance information, or (3) violations of laws and regulations, on a timely basis. A deficiency in design exists when (a) a control necessary to meet the control objective is missing or (b) an existing control is not properly designed so that, even if the control operates as designed, the control objective is not met. A deficiency in operation exists when a properly designed control does not operate as designed, or when the person performing the control does not possess the necessary authority or qualifications to perform the control effectively.

7.22 Internal auditing[93] is an important part of overall governance, accountability, and internal control. A key role of many internal audit organizations is to provide assurance that internal controls are in place to adequately mitigate risks and achieve program goals and objectives. When an assessment of internal control is needed, the auditor may use the work of the internal auditors in assessing whether internal controls are effectively designed and operating effectively, and to prevent duplication of effort. (See paragraphs 7.41 through 7.43 for standards and guidance for using the work of other auditors.)

## Information Systems Controls

7.23 Understanding information systems controls is important when information systems are used extensively throughout the program under audit and the fundamental business processes related to the audit objectives rely on information systems. Information systems controls consist of those internal controls that are dependent on information systems processing and include general controls and application controls. Information systems general controls are the policies and procedures that apply to all or a large segment of an entity's information systems. General controls help

---

[93]Many government entities identify these internal auditing activities by other names, such as inspection, appraisal, investigation, organization and methods, or management analysis. These activities assist management by reviewing selected functions.

ensure the proper operation of information systems by creating the environment for proper operation of application controls. General controls include security management, logical and physical access, configuration management, segregation of duties, and contingency planning. Application controls, sometimes referred to as business process controls, are those controls that are incorporated directly into computer applications to help ensure the validity, completeness, accuracy, and confidentiality of transactions and data during application processing. Application controls include controls over input, processing, output, master data, application interfaces, and data management system interfaces.

7.24 An organization's use of information systems controls may be extensive; however, auditors are primarily interested in those information systems controls that are significant to the audit objectives. Information systems controls are significant to the audit objectives if auditors determine that it is necessary to evaluate the effectiveness of information systems controls in order to obtain sufficient, appropriate evidence. When information systems controls are determined to be significant to the audit objectives, auditors should then evaluate the design and operating effectiveness of such controls. This evaluation would include other information systems controls that impact the effectiveness of the significant controls or the reliability of information used in performing the significant controls. Auditors should obtain a sufficient understanding of information systems controls necessary to assess audit risk and plan the audit within the context of the audit objectives.[94]

---

[94]Refer to additional criteria and guidance in *Federal Information Controls Audit Manual* (FISCAM), GAO/AIMD-12.19.6 (Washington, D.C.: January 1999) and *IS Standards, Guidelines and Procedures for Auditing and Control Professionals*, published by the Information Systems Audit and Control Association (ISACA).

**7.25** Audit procedures to evaluate the effectiveness of significant information systems controls include (1) gaining an understanding of the system as it relates to the information and (2) identifying and evaluating the general controls and application controls that are critical to providing assurance over the reliability of the information required for the audit.

**7.26** The evaluation of information systems controls may be done in conjunction with the auditors' consideration of internal control within the context of the audit objectives (see paragraphs 7.16 through 7.22), or as a separate audit objective or audit procedure, depending on the objectives of the audit. Depending on the significance of information systems controls to the audit objectives, the extent of audit procedures to obtain such an understanding may be limited or extensive. In addition, the nature and extent of audit risk related to information systems controls are affected by the nature of the hardware and software used, the configuration of the entity's systems and networks, and the entity's information systems strategy.

**7.27** Auditors should determine which audit procedures related to information systems controls are needed to obtain sufficient, appropriate evidence to support the audit findings and conclusions. The following factors may assist auditors in making this determination:

**a.** The extent to which internal controls that are significant to the audit depend on the reliability of information processed or generated by information systems.

**b.** The availability of evidence outside the information system to support the findings and conclusions: It may not be possible for auditors to obtain sufficient, appropriate evidence without evaluating the effectiveness of relevant information systems controls.

For example, if information supporting the findings and conclusions is generated by information systems or its reliability is dependent on information systems controls, there may not be sufficient supporting or corroborating information or documentary evidence that is available other than that produced by the information systems.

**c.** The relationship of information systems controls to data reliability: To obtain evidence about the reliability of computer-generated information, auditors may decide to evaluate the effectiveness of information systems controls as part of obtaining evidence about the reliability of the data. If the auditor concludes that information systems controls are effective, the auditor may reduce the extent of direct testing of data.

**d.** Evaluating the effectiveness of information systems controls as an audit objective: When evaluating the effectiveness of information systems controls is directly a part of an audit objective, auditors should test information systems controls necessary to address the audit objectives. For example, the audit may involve the effectiveness of information systems controls related to certain systems, facilities, or organizations.

## Legal and Regulatory Requirements, Provisions of Contracts or Grant Agreements, Fraud, or Abuse

### Legal and Regulatory Requirements, Contracts, and Grants

**7.28** Auditors should determine which laws, regulations, and provisions of contracts or grant agreements are significant within the context of the audit objectives and assess the risk that violations of those laws, regulations, and provisions of contracts or grant agreements could occur. Based on that risk assessment, the auditors should design and perform procedures to provide reasonable assurance of detecting instances of violations of legal and regulatory requirements or violations of provisions of contracts or grant agreements that are significant within the context of the audit objectives.

**7.29** The auditors' assessment of audit risk may be affected by such factors as the complexity or newness of the laws, regulations, and provisions of contracts or grant agreements. The auditors' assessment of audit risk also may be affected by whether the entity has controls that are effective in preventing or detecting violations of laws, regulations, and provisions of contracts or grant agreements. If auditors obtain sufficient, appropriate evidence of the effectiveness of these controls, they can reduce the extent of their tests of compliance.

Fraud

**7.30** In planning the audit, auditors should assess risks of fraud[95] occurring that is significant within the context of the audit objectives. Audit team members should discuss among the team fraud risks, including factors such as individuals' incentives or pressures to commit fraud, the opportunity for fraud to occur, and rationalizations or attitudes that could allow individuals to commit fraud. Auditors should gather and assess information to identify risks of fraud that are significant within the scope of the audit objectives or that could affect the findings and conclusions. For example, auditors may obtain information through discussion with officials of the audited entity or through other means to determine the susceptibility of the program to fraud, the status of internal controls the entity has

[95]Fraud is a type of illegal act involving the obtaining of something of value through willful misrepresentation. Whether an act is, in fact, fraud is a determination to be made through the judicial or other adjudicative system and is beyond auditors' professional responsibility.

established to detect and prevent fraud, or the risk that officials of the audited entity could override internal control. An attitude of professional skepticism in assessing these risks assists auditors in assessing which factors or risks could significantly affect the audit objectives.

**7.31** When auditors identify factors or risks related to fraud that has occurred or is likely to have occurred that they believe are significant within the context of the audit objectives, they should design procedures to provide reasonable assurance of detecting such fraud. Assessing the risk of fraud is an ongoing process throughout the audit and relates not only to planning the audit but also to evaluating evidence obtained during the audit.

**7.32** When information comes to the auditors' attention indicating that fraud that is significant within the context of the audit objectives may have occurred, auditors should extend the audit steps and procedures, as necessary, to (1) determine whether fraud has likely occurred and (2) if so, determine its effect on the audit findings. If the fraud that may have occurred is not significant within the context of the audit objectives, the auditors may conduct additional audit work as a separate engagement, or refer the matter to other parties with oversight responsibility or jurisdiction.

Abuse

**7.33** Abuse involves behavior that is deficient or improper when compared with behavior that a prudent person would consider reasonable and necessary business practice given the facts and circumstances. Abuse also includes misuse of authority or position for personal financial interests or those of an immediate or close family member or business associate. Abuse does not necessarily involve fraud, violation of laws, regulations, or provisions of a contract or grant agreement.

**7.34** If during the course of the audit, auditors become aware of abuse that could be quantitatively or qualitatively significant to the program under audit, auditors should apply audit procedures specifically directed to ascertain the potential effect on the program under audit within the context of the audit objectives. After performing additional work, auditors may discover that the abuse represents potential fraud or illegal acts. Because the determination of abuse is subjective, auditors are not required to provide reasonable assurance of detecting abuse.

## Ongoing Investigations or Legal Proceedings

**7.35** Avoiding interference with investigations or legal proceedings is important in pursuing indications of fraud, illegal acts, violations of provisions of contracts or grant agreements, or abuse. Laws, regulations, or policies might require auditors to report indications of certain types of fraud, illegal acts, violations of provisions of contracts or grant agreements, or abuse to law enforcement or investigatory authorities before performing additional audit procedures. When investigations or legal proceedings are initiated or in process, auditors should evaluate the impact on the current audit. In some cases, it may be appropriate for the auditors to work with investigators and/or legal authorities, or withdraw from or defer further work on the audit or a portion of the audit to avoid interfering with an investigation.

## Previous Audits and Attestation Engagements

**7.36** Auditors should evaluate whether the audited entity has taken appropriate corrective action to address findings and recommendations from previous engagements that are significant within the context of the audit objectives. When planning the audit, auditors should ask management of the audited entity to identify previous audits, attestation engagements, performance audits, or other studies that directly relate to the objectives of the audit, including whether related recommendations have been implemented. Auditors should use this information in assessing risk and determining the nature, timing, and extent of current audit work, including determining the extent to which testing the implementation of the corrective actions is applicable to the current audit objectives.

## Identifying Audit Criteria

**7.37** Auditors should identify criteria. Criteria represent the laws, regulations, contracts, grant agreements, standards, measures, expected performance, defined business practices, and benchmarks against which performance is compared or evaluated. Criteria identify the required or desired state or expectation with respect to the program or operation. Criteria provide a context for evaluating evidence and understanding the findings, conclusions, and recommendations included in the report. Auditors should use criteria that are relevant to the audit objectives and permit consistent assessment of the subject matter.

**7.38** The following are some examples of criteria:

**a.** purpose or goals prescribed by law or regulation or set by officials of the audited entity,

**b.** policies and procedures established by officials of the audited entity,

**c.** technically developed standards or norms,

**d.** expert opinions,

**e.** prior periods' performance,

**f.** defined business practices,

**g.** contract or grant terms, and

**h.** performance of other entities or sectors used as defined benchmarks.

## Identifying Sources of Evidence and the Amount and Type of Evidence Required

**7.39** Auditors should identify potential sources of information that could be used as evidence. Auditors should determine the amount and type of evidence needed to obtain sufficient, appropriate evidence to address the audit objectives and adequately plan audit work.

**7.40** If auditors believe that it is likely that sufficient, appropriate evidence will not be available, they may revise the audit objectives or modify the scope and methodology and determine alternative procedures to obtain additional evidence or other forms of evidence to address the current audit objectives. Auditors should also evaluate whether the lack of sufficient, appropriate evidence is due to internal control deficiencies or other program weaknesses, and whether the lack of sufficient, appropriate evidence could be the basis for audit findings. (See paragraphs 7.55 through 7.71 for standards concerning evidence.)

## Using the Work of Others

**7.41** Auditors should determine whether other auditors have conducted, or are conducting, audits of the program that could be relevant to the current audit objectives. The results of other auditors' work may be useful sources of information for planning and performing the audit. If other auditors have identified areas that warrant further audit work or follow-up, their work may influence the auditors' selection of objectives, scope, and methodology.

**7.42** If other auditors have completed audit work related to the objectives of the current audit, the current auditors may be able to use the work of the other auditors to support findings or conclusions for the current audit and, thereby, avoid duplication of efforts.

If auditors use the work of other auditors, they should perform procedures that provide a sufficient basis for using that work. Auditors should obtain evidence concerning the other auditors' qualifications and independence and should determine whether the scope, quality, and timing of the audit work performed by the other auditors is adequate for reliance in the context of the current audit objectives. Procedures that auditors may perform in making this determination include reviewing the other auditors' report, audit plan, or audit documentation, and/or performing tests of the other auditors' work. The nature and extent of evidence needed will depend on the significance of the other auditors' work to the current audit objectives and the extent to which the auditors will use that work.

**7.43** Some audits may necessitate the use of specialized techniques or methods that require the skills of a specialist. If auditors intend to use the work of specialists, they should obtain an understanding of the qualifications and independence of the specialists. (See paragraph 3.05 for independence considerations when using the work of others.) Evaluating the professional qualifications of the specialist involves the following:

**a.** the professional certification, license, or other recognition of the competence of the specialist in his or her field, as appropriate;

**b.** the reputation and standing of the specialist in the views of peers and others familiar with the specialist's capability or performance;

**c.** the specialist's experience and previous work in the subject matter; and

**d.** the auditors' prior experience in using the specialist's work.

## Assigning Staff and Other Resources

**7.44** Audit management should assign sufficient staff and specialists with adequate collective professional competence to perform the audit. (See paragraph 3.43 for a discussion of using specialists in a GAGAS audit.) Staffing an audit includes, among other things:

**a.** assigning staff and specialists with the collective knowledge, skills, and experience appropriate for the job,

**b.** assigning a sufficient number of staff and supervisors to the audit,

**c.** providing for on-the-job training of staff, and

**d.** engaging specialists when necessary.

**7.45** If planning to use the work of a specialist, auditors should document the nature and scope of the work to be performed by the specialist, including

**a.** the objectives and scope of the specialist's work,

**b.** the intended use of the specialist's work to support the audit objectives,

**c.** the specialist's procedures and findings so they can be evaluated and related to other planned audit procedures, and

**d.** the assumptions and methods used by the specialist.

## Communicating with Management, Those Charged with Governance, and Others

**7.46** Auditors should communicate an overview of the objectives, scope, and methodology, and timing of the performance audit[96] and planned reporting (including any potential restrictions on the report) to the following, as applicable:

**a.** management of the audited entity, including those with sufficient authority and responsibility to implement corrective action in the program or activity being audited;

**b.** those charged with governance;[97]

**c.** the individuals contracting for or requesting audit services, such as contracting officials, grantees; and

**d.** when auditors perform the audit pursuant to a law or regulation or they conduct the work for the legislative committee that has oversight of the audited entity, auditors should communicate with the legislative committee.

**7.47** In situations in which those charged with governance are not clearly evident, auditors should document the process followed and conclusions reached for identifying those charged with governance.

**7.48** Determining the form, content, and frequency of the communication is a matter of professional judgment, although written communication is preferred. Auditors may use an engagement letter to communicate the information. Auditors should document this communication.

---

[96]This does not apply when an element of surprise is critical to the audit objective, such as surprise audits, cash counts, or fraud-related procedures.

[97]Those charged with governance are those responsible for overseeing the strategic direction of the entity and the entity's fulfillment of its obligations related to accountability. (See appendix I, paragraphs A1.05 through A1.07.)

**7.49** If an audit is terminated before it is completed and an audit report is not issued, auditors should document the results of the work to the date of termination and why the audit was terminated. Determining whether and how to communicate the reason for terminating the audit to those charged with governance, appropriate officials of the audited entity, the entity contracting for or requesting the audit, and other appropriate officials will depend on the facts and circumstances and, therefore, is a matter of professional judgment.

## Preparing the Audit Plan

**7.50** Auditors must prepare a written audit plan for each audit. The form and content of the written audit plan may vary among audits and may include an audit strategy, audit program, project plan, audit planning paper, or other appropriate documentation of key decisions about the audit objectives, scope, and methodology and the auditors' basis for those decisions. Auditors should update the plan, as necessary, to reflect any significant changes to the plan made during the audit.

**7.51** A written audit plan provides an opportunity for the audit organization management to supervise audit planning and to determine whether

**a.** the proposed audit objectives are likely to result in a useful report,

**b.** the audit plan adequately addresses relevant risks,

**c.** the proposed audit scope and methodology are adequate to address the audit objectives,

**d.** available evidence is likely to be sufficient and appropriate for purposes of the audit, and

e. sufficient staff, supervisors, and specialists with adequate collective professional competence and other resources are available to perform the audit and to meet expected time frames for completing the work.

## Supervision

**7.52** Audit supervisors or those designated to supervise auditors must properly supervise audit staff.

**7.53** Audit supervision involves providing sufficient guidance and direction to staff assigned to the audit to address the audit objectives and follow applicable standards, while staying informed about significant problems encountered, reviewing the work performed, and providing effective on-the-job training.

**7.54** The nature and extent of the supervision of staff and the review of audit work may vary depending on a number of factors, such as the size of the audit organization, the significance of the work, and the experience of the staff.

## Obtaining Sufficient, Appropriate Evidence

**7.55** Auditors must obtain sufficient, appropriate evidence to provide a reasonable basis for their findings and conclusions.

**7.56** The concept of sufficient, appropriate evidence is integral to an audit. Appropriateness is the measure of the quality of evidence that encompasses its relevance, validity, and reliability in providing support for findings and conclusions related to the audit objectives. In assessing the overall appropriateness of evidence, auditors should assess whether the evidence is relevant, valid, and reliable. Sufficiency is a measure of the quantity of evidence used to support the findings and conclusions related to the audit objectives. In assessing the sufficiency of evidence, auditors should determine whether enough evidence has been obtained to persuade a knowledgeable person that the findings are reasonable.

**7.57** In assessing evidence, auditors should evaluate whether the evidence taken as a whole is sufficient and appropriate for addressing the audit objectives and supporting findings and conclusions. Audit objectives may vary widely, as may the level of work necessary to assess the sufficiency and appropriateness of evidence to address the objectives. For example, in establishing the appropriateness of evidence, auditors may test its reliability by obtaining supporting evidence, using statistical testing, or obtaining corroborating evidence. The concepts of audit risk and significance assist auditors with evaluating the audit evidence.

**7.58** Professional judgment assists auditors in determining the sufficiency and appropriateness of evidence taken as a whole. Interpreting, summarizing, or analyzing evidence is typically used in the process of determining the sufficiency and appropriateness of evidence and in reporting the results of the audit work. When appropriate, auditors may use statistical methods to analyze and interpret evidence to assess its sufficiency.

## Appropriateness

**7.59** Appropriateness is the measure of the quality of evidence that encompasses the relevance, validity, and reliability of evidence used for addressing the audit objectives and supporting findings and conclusions. (See appendix I, paragraph A7.03 for additional guidance regarding assessing the appropriateness of evidence in relation to the audit objectives.)

**a.** Relevance refers to the extent to which evidence has a logical relationship with, and importance to, the issue being addressed.

**b.** Validity refers to the extent to which evidence is based on sound reasoning or accurate information.

**c.** Reliability refers to the consistency of results when information is measured or tested and includes the concepts of being verifiable or supported.

**7.60** There are different types and sources of evidence that auditors may use, depending on the audit objectives. Evidence may be obtained by observation, inquiry, or inspection. Each type of evidence has its own strengths and weaknesses. (See appendix I, paragraph A7.02 for additional guidance regarding the types of evidence.) The following contrasts are useful in judging the appropriateness of evidence. However, these contrasts are not adequate in themselves to determine appropriateness. The nature and types of evidence to support auditors' findings and conclusions are matters of the auditors' professional judgment based on the audit objectives and audit risk.

**a.** Evidence obtained when internal control is effective is generally more reliable than evidence obtained when internal control is weak or nonexistent.

**b.** Evidence obtained through the auditors' direct physical examination, observation, computation, and inspection is generally more reliable than evidence obtained indirectly.

**c.** Examination of original documents is generally more reliable than examination of copies.

**d.** Testimonial evidence obtained under conditions in which persons may speak freely is generally more reliable than evidence obtained under circumstances in which the persons may be intimidated.

**e.** Testimonial evidence obtained from an individual who is not biased and has direct knowledge about the area is generally more reliable than testimonial evidence obtained from an individual who is biased or has indirect or partial knowledge about the area.

**f.** Evidence obtained from a knowledgeable, credible, and unbiased third party is generally more reliable than evidence from management of the audited entity or others who have a direct interest in the audited entity.

**7.61** Testimonial evidence may be useful in interpreting or corroborating documentary or physical information. Auditors should evaluate the objectivity, credibility, and reliability of the testimonial evidence. Documentary evidence may be used to help verify, support, or challenge testimonial evidence.

**7.62** Surveys generally provide self-reported information about existing conditions or programs. Evaluation of the survey design and administration assists auditors in evaluating the objectivity, credibility, and reliability of the self-reported information.

**7.63** When sampling is used, the method of selection that is appropriate will depend on the audit objectives. When a representative sample is needed, the use of statistical sampling approaches generally results in stronger evidence than that obtained from nonstatistical techniques. When a representative sample is not needed, a targeted selection may be effective if the auditors have isolated certain risk factors or other criteria to target the selection.

**7.64** When auditors use information gathered by officials of the audited entity as part of their evidence, they should determine what the officials of the audited entity or other auditors did to obtain assurance over the reliability of the information. The auditor may find it necessary to perform testing of management's procedures to obtain assurance or perform direct testing of the information. The nature and extent of the auditors' procedures will depend on the significance of the information to the audit objectives and the nature of the information being used.

**7.65** Auditors should assess the sufficiency and appropriateness of computer-processed information regardless of whether this information is provided to auditors or auditors independently extract it. The nature, timing, and extent of audit procedures to assess sufficiency and appropriateness is affected by the effectiveness of the entity's internal controls over the information, including information systems controls, and the significance of the information and the level of detail presented in the auditors' findings and conclusions in light of the audit objectives. (See paragraphs 7.23 through 7.27 for additional discussion on assessing the effectiveness of information systems controls.)

## Sufficiency

**7.66** Sufficiency is a measure of the quantity of evidence used for addressing the audit objectives and supporting findings and conclusions. Sufficiency also depends on the appropriateness of the evidence. In determining the sufficiency of evidence, auditors should determine whether enough appropriate evidence exists to address the audit objectives and support the findings and conclusions.

**7.67** The following presumptions are useful in judging the sufficiency of evidence. The sufficiency of evidence required to support the auditors' findings and conclusions is a matter of the auditors' professional judgment.

**a.** The greater the audit risk, the greater the quantity and quality of evidence required.

**b.** Stronger evidence may allow less evidence to be used.

**c.** Having a large volume of audit evidence does not compensate for a lack of relevance, validity, or reliability.

## Overall Assessment of Evidence

**7.68** Auditors should determine the overall sufficiency and appropriateness of evidence to provide a reasonable basis for the findings and conclusions, within the context of the audit objectives. Professional judgments about the sufficiency and appropriateness of evidence are closely interrelated, as auditors interpret the results of audit testing and evaluate whether the nature and extent of the evidence obtained is sufficient and appropriate. Auditors should perform and document an overall assessment of the collective evidence used to support findings and conclusions, including the results of any specific assessments conducted to conclude on the validity and reliability of specific evidence.

**7.69** Sufficiency and appropriateness of evidence are relative concepts, which may be thought of in terms of a continuum rather than as absolutes. Sufficiency and appropriateness are evaluated in the context of the related findings and conclusions. For example, even though the auditors may have some limitations or uncertainties about the sufficiency or appropriateness of some of the evidence, they may nonetheless determine that in total there is sufficient, appropriate evidence to support the findings and conclusions.

**7.70** When assessing the sufficiency and appropriateness of evidence, auditors should evaluate the expected significance of evidence to the audit objectives, findings, and conclusions, available corroborating evidence, and the level of audit risk. The steps to assess evidence may depend on the nature of the evidence, how the evidence is used in the audit or report, and the audit objectives.

**a.** Evidence is sufficient and appropriate when it provides a reasonable basis for supporting the findings or conclusions within the context of the audit objectives.

**b.** Evidence is not sufficient or not appropriate when (1) using the evidence carries an unacceptably high risk that it could lead to an incorrect or improper conclusion, (2) the evidence has significant limitations, given the audit objectives and intended use of the evidence, or (3) the evidence does not provide an adequate basis for addressing the audit objectives or supporting the findings and conclusions. Auditors should not use such evidence as support for findings and conclusions.

**7.71** Evidence has limitations or uncertainties when the validity or reliability of the evidence has not been assessed or cannot be assessed, given the audit objectives and the intended use of the evidence. Limitations also include errors identified by the auditors in their testing. When the auditors identify limitations or uncertainties in evidence that is significant to the audit findings and conclusions, they should apply additional procedures, as appropriate. Such procedures include

**a.** seeking independent, corroborating evidence from other sources;

**b.** redefining the audit objectives or limiting the audit scope to eliminate the need to use the evidence;

**c.** presenting the findings and conclusions so that the supporting evidence is sufficient and appropriate and describing in the report the limitations or uncertainties with the validity or reliability of the evidence, if such disclosure is necessary to avoid misleading the report users about the findings or conclusions (see paragraph 8.15 for additional reporting requirements when there are limitations or uncertainties with the validity or reliability of evidence); or

**d.** determining whether to report the limitations or uncertainties as a finding, including any related, significant internal control deficiencies.

## Developing Elements of a Finding

**7.72** Auditors should plan and perform procedures to develop the elements of a finding necessary to address the audit objectives. In addition, if auditors are able to sufficiently develop the elements of a finding, they should develop recommendations for corrective action if they are significant within the context of the audit objectives. The elements needed for a finding depend entirely on the objectives of the audit. Thus, a finding or set of findings is complete to the extent that the audit objectives are addressed and the report clearly relates those objectives to the elements of a finding. For example, an audit objective may be limited to determining the current status or condition of program operations or progress in implementing legislative requirements, and not the related cause or effect. In this situation, developing the condition would address the audit objective and development of the other elements of a finding would not be necessary.

**7.73** The element of criteria is discussed in paragraphs 7.37 and 7.38, and the other elements of a finding— condition, effect, and cause--are discussed in paragraphs 7.74 through 7.76.

**7.74** Condition: Condition is a situation that exists. The condition is determined and documented during the audit.

**7.75** Cause: The cause identifies the reason or explanation for the condition or the factor or factors responsible for the difference between the situation that exists (condition) and the required or desired state (criteria), which may also serve as a basis for recommendations for corrective actions. Common factors include poorly designed policies, procedures, or criteria; inconsistent, incomplete, or incorrect implementation; or factors beyond the control of program management. Auditors may assess whether the evidence provides a reasonable and convincing argument for why the stated cause is the key factor or factors contributing to the difference. When the audit objectives include explaining why a particular type of positive or negative program performance, output, or outcome identified in the audit occurred, they are referred to as "cause." Identifying the cause of problems may assist auditors in making constructive recommendations for correction. Because problems can result from a number of plausible factors or multiple causes, the recommendation can be more persuasive if auditors can clearly demonstrate and explain with evidence and reasoning the link between the problems and the factor or factors they have identified as the cause or causes. Auditors may identify deficiencies in program design or structure as the cause of deficient performance. Auditors may also identify deficiencies in internal control that are significant to the subject matter of the performance audit as the cause of deficient performance. In developing these types of findings, the deficiencies in program design or internal control would be described as the "cause." Often the causes of deficient program performance are complex and involve multiple factors, including fundamental, systemic root causes. Alternatively, when the audit objectives include estimating the program's effect on changes in physical,

social, or economic conditions, auditors seek evidence
of the extent to which the program itself is the "cause"
of those changes.

**7.76** Effect or potential effect: The effect is a clear,
logical link to establish the impact or potential impact of
the difference between the situation that exists
(condition) and the required or desired state (criteria).
The effect or potential effect identifies the outcomes or
consequences of the condition. When the audit
objectives include identifying the actual or potential
consequences of a condition that varies (either
positively or negatively) from the criteria identified in
the audit, "effect" is a measure of those consequences.
Effect or potential effect may be used to demonstrate
the need for corrective action in response to identified
problems or relevant risks. When the audit objectives
include estimating the extent to which a program has
caused changes in physical, social, or economic
conditions, "effect" is a measure of the impact achieved
by the program. In this case, effect is the extent to which
positive or negative changes in actual physical, social, or
economic conditions can be identified and attributed to
the program.

# Audit Documentation

**7.77** Auditors must prepare audit documentation related
to planning, conducting, and reporting for each audit.
Auditors should prepare audit documentation in
sufficient detail to enable an experienced auditor,[98]
having no previous connection to the audit, to

---

[98]An experienced auditor means an individual (whether internal or
external to the audit organization) who possesses the competencies
and skills that would have enabled him or her to perform the
performance audit. These competencies and skills include an
understanding of (1) the performance audit processes, (2) GAGAS and
applicable legal and regulatory requirements, (3) the subject matter
associated with achieving the audit objectives, and (4) issues related
to the audited entity's environment.

understand from the audit documentation the nature, timing, extent, and results of audit procedures performed, the audit evidence obtained and its source and the conclusions reached, including evidence that supports the auditors' significant judgments and conclusions. Auditors should prepare audit documentation that contains support for findings, conclusions, and recommendations before they issue their report.

**7.78** Auditors should design the form and content of audit documentation to meet the circumstances of the particular audit. The audit documentation constitutes the principal record of the work that the auditors have performed in accordance with standards and the conclusions that the auditors have reached. The quantity, type, and content of audit documentation are a matter of the auditors' professional judgment.

**7.79** Audit documentation is an essential element of audit quality. The process of preparing and reviewing audit documentation contributes to the quality of an audit. Audit documentation serves to (1) provide the principal support for the auditors' report, (2) aid auditors in conducting and supervising the audit, and (3) allow for the review of audit quality.

**7.80** Under GAGAS, auditors should document the following:

**a.** the objectives, scope, and methodology of the audit;

**b.** the work performed to support significant judgments and conclusions, including descriptions of transactions and records examined;[99] and

**c.** evidence of supervisory review, before the audit report is issued, of the work performed that supports findings, conclusions, and recommendations contained in the audit report.

**7.81** When auditors do not comply with applicable GAGAS requirements due to law, regulation, scope limitations, restrictions on access to records, or other issues impacting the audit, the auditors should document the departure from the GAGAS requirements and the impact on the audit and on the auditors' conclusions. This applies to departures from both mandatory requirements and presumptively mandatory requirements when alternative procedures performed in the circumstances were not sufficient to achieve the objectives of the standard. (See paragraphs 1.12 and 1.13.)

**7.82** Audit organizations should establish policies and procedures for the safe custody and retention of audit documentation for a time sufficient to satisfy legal, regulatory, and administrative requirements for records retention. Whether audit documentation is in paper, electronic, or other media, the integrity, accessibility, and retrievability of the underlying information could be compromised if the documentation is altered, added to, or deleted without the auditors' knowledge, or if the documentation is lost or damaged. For audit documentation that is retained electronically, the audit

---

[99]Auditors may meet this requirement by listing file numbers, case numbers, or other means of identifying specific documents they examined. They are not required to include copies of documents they examined as part of the audit documentation, nor are they required to list detailed information from those documents.

organization should establish information systems controls concerning accessing and updating the audit documentation.

**7.83** Underlying GAGAS audits is the premise that audit organizations in federal, state, and local governments and public accounting firms engaged to perform audits in accordance with GAGAS cooperate in auditing programs of common interest so that auditors may use others' work and avoid duplication of efforts. Subject to applicable laws and regulations, auditors should make appropriate individuals, as well as audit documentation, available upon request and in a timely manner to other auditors or reviewers to satisfy these objectives. The use of auditors' work by other auditors may be facilitated by contractual arrangements for GAGAS audits that provide for full and timely access to appropriate individuals, as well as audit documentation.

**7.84** Audit organizations should develop policies to deal with requests by outside parties to obtain access to audit documentation, especially when an outside party attempts to obtain information indirectly through the auditor rather than directly from the audited entity. In developing such policies, audit organizations should determine what laws and regulations apply, if any.

# Chapter 8

# Reporting Standards for Performance Audits

## Introduction

**8.01** This chapter establishes reporting standards and provides guidance for performance audits conducted in accordance with generally accepted government auditing standards (GAGAS). The reporting standards for performance audits relate to the form of the report, the report contents, and report issuance and distribution.

**8.02** For performance audits performed in accordance with GAGAS, chapters 1 through 3 and 7 and 8 apply.

## Reporting

**8.03** Auditors must issue audit reports communicating the results of each completed performance audit.

**8.04** Auditors should use a form of the audit report that is appropriate for its intended use and is in writing or in some other retrievable form. (See paragraph 8.42 for situations when audit organizations are subject to public records laws.) For example, auditors may present audit reports using electronic media that are retrievable by report users and the audit organization. The users' needs will influence the form of the audit report. Different forms of audit reports include written reports, letters, briefing slides, or other presentation materials.

**8.05** The purposes of audit reports are to (1) communicate the results of audits to those charged with governance, the appropriate officials of the audited entity, and the appropriate oversight officials; (2) make the results less susceptible to misunderstanding; (3) make the results available to the public, as applicable (see paragraph 8.39 for additional guidance on classified or limited use reports and paragraph 8.43b for distribution of reports for internal auditors); and (4) facilitate follow-up to determine whether appropriate corrective actions have been taken.

**8.06** If an audit is terminated before it is completed and an audit report is not issued, auditors should follow the guidance in paragraph 7.49.

**8.07** If after the report is issued, the auditors discover that they did not have sufficient, appropriate evidence to support the reported findings or conclusions, they should communicate with those charged with governance, the appropriate officials of the audited entity, and the appropriate officials of the organizations requiring or arranging for the audits, so that they do not continue to rely on the findings or conclusions that were not supported. If the report was previously posted to the auditors' publicly accessible website, the auditors should remove the report and post a public notification that the report was removed. The auditors should then determine whether to conduct additional audit work necessary to reissue the report with revised findings or conclusions.

## Report Contents

**8.08** Auditors should prepare audit reports that contain (1) the objectives, scope, and methodology of the audit; (2) the audit results, including findings, conclusions, and recommendations, as appropriate; (3) a statement about the auditors' compliance with GAGAS; (4) a summary of the views of responsible officials; and (5) if applicable, the nature of any confidential or sensitive information omitted.

## Objectives, Scope, and Methodology

**8.09** Auditors should include in the report a description of the audit objectives and the scope and methodology used for addressing the audit objectives. Report users need this information to understand the purpose of the audit, the nature and extent of the audit work performed, the context and perspective regarding what is reported, and any significant limitations in audit objectives, scope, or methodology.

**8.10** Audit objectives for performance audits may vary widely. Auditors should communicate audit objectives in the audit report in a clear, specific, neutral, and unbiased manner that includes relevant assumptions, including why the audit organization undertook the assignment and the underlying purpose of the audit and resulting report. When audit objectives are limited and broader objectives can be inferred by users, stating in the audit report that certain issues were outside the scope of the audit can avoid potential misunderstanding.

**8.11** Auditors should describe the scope of the work performed and any limitations, including issues that would be relevant to likely users, so that they could reasonably interpret the findings, conclusions, and recommendations in the report without being misled. Auditors should also report any significant constraints imposed on the audit approach by information limitations or scope impairments, including denials of access to certain records or individuals.

**8.12** In describing the work conducted to address the audit objectives and support the reported findings and conclusions, auditors should, as applicable, explain the relationship between the population and the items tested; identify organizations, geographic locations, and the period covered; report the kinds and sources of evidence; and explain any significant limitations or uncertainties based on the auditors' overall assessment of the sufficiency and appropriateness of the evidence in the aggregate.

**8.13** In reporting audit methodology, auditors should explain how the completed audit work supports the audit objectives, including the evidence gathering and analysis techniques, in sufficient detail to allow knowledgeable users of their reports to understand how the auditors addressed the audit objectives. When the auditors used extensive or multiple sources of information, the auditors may include a description of the procedures performed as part of their assessment of the sufficiency and appropriateness of information used as audit evidence. Auditors should identify significant assumptions made in conducting the audit; describe comparative techniques applied; describe the criteria used; and, when sampling significantly supports the auditors' findings, conclusions, or recommendations, describe the sample design and state why the design was chosen, including whether the results can be projected to the intended population.

## Reporting Findings

**8.14** In the audit report, auditors should present sufficient, appropriate evidence to support the findings and conclusions in relation to the audit objectives. Clearly developed findings, as discussed in paragraphs 7.72 through 7.76, assist management or oversight officials of the audited entity in understanding the need for taking corrective action. If auditors are able to sufficiently develop the elements of a finding, they should provide recommendations for corrective action if they are significant within the context of the audit objectives. However, the extent to which the elements for a finding are developed depends on the audit objectives. Thus, a finding or set of findings is complete to the extent that the auditors address the audit objectives.

**8.15** Auditors should describe in their report limitations or uncertainties with the reliability or validity of evidence if (1) the evidence is significant to the findings and conclusions within the context of the audit objectives and (2) such disclosure is necessary to avoid misleading the report users about the findings and conclusions. As discussed in chapter 7, even though the auditors may have some uncertainty about the sufficiency or appropriateness of some of the evidence, they may nonetheless determine that in total there is sufficient, appropriate evidence given the findings and conclusions. Auditors should describe the limitations or uncertainties regarding evidence in conjunction with the findings and conclusions, in addition to describing those limitations or uncertainties as part of the objectives, scope, and methodology. Additionally, this description provides report users with a clear understanding regarding how much responsibility the auditors are taking for the information.

**8.16** Auditors should place their findings in perspective by describing the nature and extent of the issues being reported and the extent of the work performed that resulted in the finding. To give the reader a basis for judging the prevalence and consequences of these findings, auditors should, as applicable, relate the instances identified to the population or the number of cases examined and quantify the results in terms of dollar value, or other measures, as appropriate. If the results cannot be projected, auditors should limit their conclusions appropriately.

**8.17** Auditors may provide selective background information to establish the context for the overall message and to help the reader understand the findings and significance of the issues discussed.[100] When reporting on the results of their work, auditors should disclose significant facts relevant to the objectives of their work and known to them which, if not disclosed, could mislead knowledgeable users, misrepresent the results, or conceal significant improper or illegal practices.

---

[100]Appropriate background information may include information on how programs and operations work; the significance of programs and operations (e.g., dollars, impact, purposes, and past audit work, if relevant); a description of the audited entity's responsibilities; and explanation of terms, organizational structure, and the statutory basis for the program and operations.

**8.18** Auditors should report deficiencies[101] in internal control that are significant within the context of the objectives of the audit, all instances of fraud, illegal acts[102] unless they are inconsequential within the context of the audit objectives, significant violations of provisions of contracts or grant agreements, and significant abuse that have occurred or are likely to have occurred.

Deficiencies in Internal Control

**8.19** Auditors should include in the audit report (1) the scope of their work on internal control and (2) any deficiencies in internal control that are significant within the context of the audit objectives and based upon the audit work performed. When auditors detect deficiencies in internal control that are not significant to the objectives of the audit, they may include those deficiencies in the report or communicate those deficiencies in writing to officials of the audited entity unless the deficiencies are inconsequential considering both qualitative and quantitative factors. Auditors should refer to that written communication in the audit report, if the written communication is separate from the audit report. Determining whether or how to communicate to officials of the audited entity deficiencies that are inconsequential within the context of the audit objectives is a matter of professional judgment. Auditors should document such communications.

---

[101]As discussed in paragraph 7.21, in performance audits, a deficiency in internal control exists when the design or operation of a control does not allow management or employees, in the normal course of performing their assigned functions, to prevent or detect (1) misstatements in financial or performance information, (2) violations of laws and regulations, or (3) impairments of effectiveness or efficiency of operations, on a timely basis.

[102]Whether a particular act is, in fact, illegal may have to await final determination by a court of law or other adjudicative body. Disclosing matters that have led auditors to conclude that an illegal act is likely to have occurred is not a final determination of illegality.

**8.20** In a performance audit, auditors may conclude that identified deficiencies in internal control that are significant within the context of the audit objectives are the cause of deficient performance of the program or operations being audited. In reporting this type of finding, the internal control deficiency would be described as the cause.

Fraud, Illegal Acts, Violations of Provisions of Contracts or Grant Agreements, and Abuse

**8.21** When auditors conclude, based on sufficient, appropriate evidence, that fraud, illegal acts, significant violations of provisions of contracts or grant agreements, or significant abuse either has occurred or is likely to have occurred, they should report the matter as a finding.

**8.22** When auditors detect violations of provisions of contracts or grant agreements, or abuse that are not significant, they should communicate those findings in writing to officials of the audited entity unless the findings are inconsequential within the context of the audit objectives, considering both qualitative and quantitative factors. Determining whether or how to communicate to officials of the audited entity fraud, illegal acts, violations of provisions of contracts or grant agreements, or abuse that is inconsequential is a matter of the auditors' professional judgment. Auditors should document such communications.

**8.23** When fraud, illegal acts, violations of provisions of contracts or grant agreements, or abuse either have occurred or are likely to have occurred, auditors may consult with authorities or legal counsel about whether publicly reporting such information would compromise investigative or legal proceedings. Auditors may limit their public reporting to matters that would not compromise those proceedings, and for example, report only on information that is already a part of the public record.

Reporting Findings
Directly to Parties
Outside the Audited
Entity

**8.24** Auditors should report known or likely fraud, illegal acts, violations of provisions of contracts or grant agreements, or abuse directly to parties outside the audited entity in the following two circumstances.[103]

**a.** When entity management fails to satisfy legal or regulatory requirements to report such information to external parties specified in law or regulation, auditors should first communicate the failure to report such information to those charged with governance. If the audited entity still does not report this information to the specified external parties as soon as practicable after the auditors' communication with those charged with governance, then the auditors should report the information directly to the specified external parties.

**b.** When entity management fails to take timely and appropriate steps to respond to known or likely fraud, illegal acts, violations of provisions of contracts or grant agreements, or abuse that (1) is significant to the findings and conclusions, and (2) involves funding received directly or indirectly from a government agency, auditors should first report management's failure to take timely and appropriate steps to those charged with governance. If the audited entity still does not take timely and appropriate steps as soon as practicable after the auditors' communication with those charged with governance, then the auditors should report the entity's failure to take timely and appropriate steps directly to the funding agency.

**8.25** The reporting in paragraph 8.24 is in addition to any legal requirements to report such information directly to parties outside the audited entity. Auditors

---

[103]Internal audit organizations do not have a duty to report outside the entity unless required by law, rule, regulation, or policy. (See paragraph 8.43b for reporting standards for internal audit organizations when reporting externally.)

should comply with these requirements even if they
have resigned or been dismissed from the audit prior to
its completion.

**8.26** Auditors should obtain sufficient, appropriate
evidence, such as confirmation from outside parties, to
corroborate assertions by management of the audited
entity that it has reported such findings in accordance
with laws, regulations, and funding agreements. When
auditors are unable to do so, they should report such
information directly as discussed in paragraph 8.24.

## Conclusions

**8.27** Auditors should report conclusions, as applicable,
based on the audit objectives and the audit findings.
Report conclusions are logical inferences about the
program based on the auditors' findings, not merely a
summary of the findings. The strength of the auditors'
conclusions depends on the sufficiency and
appropriateness of the evidence supporting the findings
and the soundness of the logic used to formulate the
conclusions. Conclusions are stronger if they lead to the
auditors' recommendations and convince the
knowledgeable user of the report that action is
necessary.

## Recommendations

**8.28** Auditors should recommend actions to correct
problems identified during the audit and to improve
programs and operations when the potential for
improvement in programs, operations, and performance
is substantiated by the reported findings and
conclusions. Auditors should make recommendations
that flow logically from the findings and conclusions, are
directed at resolving the cause of identified problems,
and clearly state the actions recommended.

**8.29** Effective recommendations encourage
improvements in the conduct of government programs
and operations. Recommendations are effective when

they are addressed to parties that have the authority to
act and when the recommended actions are specific,
practical, cost effective, and measurable.

## Reporting Auditors' Compliance with GAGAS

**8.30** When auditors comply with all applicable GAGAS
requirements, they should use the following language,
which represents an unmodified GAGAS compliance
statement, in the audit report to indicate that they
performed the audit in accordance with GAGAS. (See
paragraphs 1.12 and 1.13.)

We conducted this performance audit in accordance
with generally accepted government auditing standards.
Those standards require that we plan and perform the
audit to obtain sufficient, appropriate evidence to
provide a reasonable basis for our findings and
conclusions based on our audit objectives. We believe
that the evidence obtained provides a reasonable basis
for our findings and conclusions based on our audit
objectives.

**8.31** When auditors do not comply with all applicable
GAGAS requirements, they should include a modified
GAGAS compliance statement in the audit report. For
performance audits, auditors should use a statement
that includes either (1) the language in 8.30, modified to
indicate the standards that were not followed or
(2) language that the auditor did not follow GAGAS.
(See paragraphs 1.12 and 1.13 for additional standards
on citing compliance with GAGAS.)

## Reporting Views of Responsible Officials

**8.32** Providing a draft report with findings for review
and comment by responsible officials of the audited
entity and others helps the auditors develop a report
that is fair, complete, and objective. Including the views
of responsible officials results in a report that presents
not only the auditors' findings, conclusions, and
recommendations, but also the perspectives of the

responsible officials of the audited entity and the corrective actions they plan to take. Obtaining the comments in writing is preferred, but oral comments are acceptable.

**8.33** When auditors receive written comments from the responsible officials, they should include in their report a copy of the officials' written comments, or a summary of the comments received. When the responsible officials provide oral comments only, auditors should prepare a summary of the oral comments and provide a copy of the summary to the responsible officials to verify that the comments are accurately stated.

**8.34** Auditors should also include in the report an evaluation of the comments, as appropriate. In cases in which the audited entity provides technical comments in addition to its written or oral comments on the report, auditors may disclose in the report that such comments were received.

**8.35** Obtaining oral comments may be appropriate when, for example, there is a reporting date critical to meeting a user's needs; auditors have worked closely with the responsible officials throughout the conduct of the work and the parties are familiar with the findings and issues addressed in the draft report; or the auditors do not expect major disagreements with the findings, conclusions, and recommendations in the draft report, or major controversies with regard to the issues discussed in the draft report.

**8.36** When the audited entity's comments are inconsistent or in conflict with the findings, conclusions, or recommendations in the draft report, or when planned corrective actions do not adequately address the auditors' recommendations, the auditors should evaluate the validity of the audited entity's comments. If the auditors disagree with the comments, they should

explain in the report their reasons for disagreement.
Conversely, the auditors should modify their report as
necessary if they find the comments valid and supported
with sufficient, appropriate evidence.

**8.37** If the audited entity refuses to provide comments
or is unable to provide comments within a reasonable
period of time, the auditors may issue the report without
receiving comments from the audited entity. In such
cases, the auditors should indicate in the report that the
audited entity did not provide comments.

## Reporting Confidential or Sensitive Information

**8.38** If certain pertinent information is prohibited from
public disclosure or is excluded from a report due to the
confidential or sensitive nature of the information,
auditors should disclose in the report that certain
information has been omitted and the reason or other
circumstances that makes the omission necessary.

**8.39** Certain information may be classified or may be
otherwise prohibited from general disclosure by federal,
state, or local laws or regulations. In such
circumstances, auditors may issue a separate, classified
or limited use report containing such information and
distribute the report only to persons authorized by law
or regulation to receive it.

**8.40** Additional circumstances associated with public
safety and security concerns could also justify the
exclusion of certain information from a publicly
available or widely distributed report. For example,
detailed information related to computer security for a
particular program may be excluded from publicly
available reports because of the potential damage that
could be caused by the misuse of this information. In
such circumstances, auditors may issue a limited use
report containing such information and distribute the
report only to those parties responsible for acting on the

auditors' recommendations. The auditors may consult with legal counsel regarding any requirements or other circumstances that may necessitate the omission of certain information.

**8.41** Considering the broad public interest in the program or activity under review assists auditors when deciding whether to exclude certain information from publicly available reports. When circumstances call for omission of certain information, auditors should evaluate whether this omission could distort the audit results or conceal improper or illegal practices.

**8.42** When audit organizations are subject to public records laws, auditors should determine whether public records laws could impact the availability of classified or limited use reports and determine whether other means of communicating with management and those charged with governance would be more appropriate. For example, the auditors may communicate general information in a written report and communicate detailed information verbally. The auditor may consult with legal counsel regarding applicable public records laws.

## Distributing Reports

**8.43** Distribution of reports completed under GAGAS depends on the relationship of the auditors to the audited organization and the nature of the information contained in the report. If the subject of the audit involves material that is classified for security purposes or contains confidential or sensitive information, auditors may limit the report distribution. (See paragraphs 8.38 through 8.42 for additional guidance on limited report distribution.) Auditors should document any limitation on report distribution. The following discussion outlines distribution for reports completed under GAGAS:

**a.** Audit organizations in government entities should distribute audit reports to those charged with governance, to the appropriate officials of the audited entity, and to the appropriate oversight bodies or organizations requiring or arranging for the audits. As appropriate, auditors should also distribute copies of the reports to other officials who have legal oversight authority or who may be responsible for acting on audit findings and recommendations, and to others authorized to receive such reports.

**b.** Internal audit organizations in government entities may follow the Institute of Internal Auditors (IIA) *International Standards for the Professional Practice of Internal Auditing.* Under GAGAS and IIA standards, the head of the internal audit organization should communicate results to parties who can ensure that the results are given due consideration. If not otherwise mandated by statutory or regulatory requirements, prior to releasing results to parties outside the organization, the head of the internal audit organization should: (1) assess the potential risk to the organization, (2) consult with senior management and/or legal counsel as appropriate, and (3) control dissemination by indicating the intended users of the report.

**c.** Public accounting firms contracted to perform an audit under GAGAS should clarify report distribution responsibilities with the engaging organization. If the contracted firm is to make the distribution, it should reach agreement with the party contracting for the audit about which officials or organizations will receive the report and the steps being taken to make the report available to the public.

# Supplemental Guidance

## Introduction

**A.01** The following sections provide supplemental guidance for auditors and the audited entities to assist in the implementation of generally accepted government auditing standards (GAGAS). The guidance does not establish additional requirements but instead is intended to facilitate auditor implementation of GAGAS in chapters 1 through 8. The supplemental guidance in the first section may be of assistance for all types of audits and engagements covered by GAGAS. Subsequent sections provide supplemental guidance for specific chapters of GAGAS, as indicated.

## Overall Supplemental Guidance

**A.02** Chapters 4 through 8 discuss the field work and reporting standards for financial audits, attestation engagements, and performance audits. The identification of significant deficiencies in internal control, significant abuse, fraud risks, illegal acts, and significant violations of provisions of contracts or grant agreements are important aspects of government auditing. The following discussion is provided to assist auditors in identifying significant deficiencies in internal control, abuse, and indicators of fraud risk and to assist auditors in determining whether illegal acts and violations of provisions of contracts or grant agreements are significant within the context of the audit objectives.

## Examples of Deficiencies in Internal Control

**A.03** GAGAS contain requirements for reporting identified deficiencies in internal control.

- For financial audits, see paragraphs 5.10 through 5.14.

- For attestation engagements, see paragraphs 6.33 through 6.35.

- For performance audits, see paragraphs 8.18 through 8.20.

**A.04** The following are examples of control deficiencies:

**a.** Insufficient control consciousness within the organization, for example the tone at the top and the control environment. Control deficiencies in other components of internal control could lead the auditor to conclude that weaknesses exist in the control environment.

**b.** Ineffective oversight by those charged with governance of the entity's financial reporting, performance reporting, or internal control, or an ineffective overall governance structure.

**c.** Control systems that did not prevent or detect material misstatements so that it was later necessary to restate previously issued financial statements or operational results. Control systems that did not prevent or detect material misstatements in performance or operational results so that it was later necessary to make significant corrections to those results.

**d.** Control systems that did not prevent or detect material misstatements identified by the auditor. This includes misstatements involving estimation and judgment for which the auditor identifies potential material adjustments and corrections of the recorded amounts.

**e.** An ineffective internal audit function or risk assessment function at an entity for which such functions are important to the monitoring or risk assessment component of internal control, such as for a very large or highly complex entity.

**f.** Identification of fraud of any magnitude on the part of senior management.

**g.** Failure by management or those charged with governance to assess the effect of a significant deficiency previously communicated to them and either to correct it or to conclude that it will not be corrected.

**h.** Inadequate controls for the safeguarding of assets.

**i.** Evidence of intentional override of internal control by those in authority to the detriment of the overall objectives of the system.

**j.** Deficiencies in the design or operation of internal control that could result in violations of laws, regulations, provisions of contracts or grant agreements, fraud, or abuse having a direct and material effect on the financial statements or the audit objective.

**k.** Inadequate design of information systems general and application controls that prevent the information system from providing complete and accurate information consistent with financial or performance reporting objectives and other current needs.

**l.** Failure of an application control caused by a deficiency in the design or operation of an information systems general control.

**m.** Employees or management who lack the qualifications and training to fulfill their assigned functions.

## Examples of Abuse

**A.05** GAGAS contain requirements for responding to indications of material abuse and reporting abuse that is material to the audit objectives.

- For financial audits, see paragraphs 4.12 and 4.13 and paragraphs 5.15 through 5.17.

- For attestation engagements, see paragraphs 6.13c and 6.14 and paragraphs 6.36c through 6.38.

- For performance audits, see paragraphs 7.33 and 7.34 and paragraphs 8.21 through 8.23.

**A.06** The following are examples of abuse, depending on the facts and circumstances:

**a.** Creating unneeded overtime.

**b.** Requesting staff to perform personal errands or work tasks for a supervisor or manager.

**c.** Misusing the official's position for personal gain (including actions that could be perceived by an objective third party with knowledge of the relevant information as improperly benefiting an official's personal financial interests or those of an immediate or close family member; a general partner; an organization for which the official serves as an officer, director, trustee, or employee; or an organization with which the official is negotiating concerning future employment).

**d.** Making travel choices that are contrary to existing travel policies or are unnecessarily extravagant or expensive.

**e.** Making procurement or vendor selections that are contrary to existing policies or are unnecessarily extravagant or expensive.

| Examples of Indicators of Fraud Risk | **A.07** GAGAS contain requirements relating to evaluating fraud risk. |

- For financial audits, see paragraphs 4.27 and 4.28 and paragraphs 5.15 through 5.17.

- For attestation engagements, see paragraphs 6.13a and b and paragraphs 6.36 through 6.38.

- For performance audits, see paragraphs 7.30 through 7.32 and paragraphs 8.21 through 8.23.

**A.08** In some circumstances, conditions such as the following might indicate a heightened risk of fraud:

**a.** the entity's financial stability, viability, or budget is threatened by economic, programmatic, or entity operating conditions;

**b.** the nature of the audited entity's operations provide opportunities to engage in fraud;

**c.** inadequate monitoring by management for compliance with policies, laws, and regulations;

**d.** the organizational structure is unstable or unnecessarily complex;

**e.** lack of communication and/or support for ethical standards by management;

**f.** management has a willingness to accept unusually high levels of risk in making significant decisions;

**g.** a history of impropriety, such as previous issues with fraud, waste, abuse, or questionable practices, or past audits or investigations with findings of questionable or criminal activity;

**h.** operating policies and procedures have not been developed or are outdated;

**i.** key documentation is lacking or does not exist;

**j.** lack of asset accountability or safeguarding procedures;

**k.** improper payments;

**l.** false or misleading information;

**m.** a pattern of large procurements in any budget line with remaining funds at year end, in order to "use up all of the funds available"; and

**n.** unusual patterns and trends in contracting, procurement, acquisition, and other activities of the entity or program under audit.

# Determining Whether Laws, Regulations, or Provisions of Contracts or Grant Agreements Are Significant within the Context of the Audit Objectives

**A.09** GAGAS contain requirements for determining whether laws, regulations, or provisions of contracts or grant agreements are significant within the context of the audit objectives.

- For financial audits, see paragraphs 4.10 and 4.11.

- For attestation engagements, see paragraphs 6.13a and b.

- For performance audits, see paragraphs 7.28 and 7.29.

**A.10** Government programs are subject to many laws, regulations, and provisions of contracts or grant agreements. At the same time, their significance within the context of the audit objectives varies widely, depending on the objectives of the audit. Auditors may find the following approach helpful in assessing whether laws, regulations, or provisions of contracts or grant agreements are significant within the context of the audit objectives:

**a.** Express each audit objective in terms of questions about specific aspects of the program being audited (that is, purpose and goals, internal control, inputs, program operations, outputs, and outcomes).

**b.** Identify laws, regulations, and provisions of contracts or grant agreements that directly relate to specific aspects of the program within the context of the audit objectives.

**c.** Determine if the audit objectives or the auditors' conclusions could be significantly affected if violations of those laws, regulations, or provisions of contracts or grant agreements occurred. If the audit objectives or audit conclusions could be significantly affected, then those laws, regulations, and provisions of contracts or grant agreements are likely to be significant to the audit objectives.

**A.11** Auditors may consult with either their own or management's legal counsel to (1) determine those laws and regulations that are significant to the audit objectives, (2) design tests of compliance with laws and regulations, or (3) evaluate the results of those tests. Auditors also may consult with either their own or management's legal counsel when audit objectives require testing compliance with provisions of contracts or grant agreements. Depending on the circumstances of the audit, auditors may consult with others, such as investigative staff, other audit organizations or government entities that provided professional services to the audited entity, or applicable law enforcement authorities, to obtain information on compliance matters.

# Information to Accompany Chapter 1

**A1.01** Chapter 1 discusses the use and application of GAGAS and the role of auditing in government accountability. Those charged with governance and management of audited organizations also have roles in government accountability. The discussion that follows is provided to assist auditors in understanding the roles of others in accountability. The following section also contains background information on the laws, regulations, and guidelines that require the use of GAGAS. This information is provided to place GAGAS within the context of overall government accountability.

## Laws, Regulations, and Guidelines That Require Use of GAGAS

**A1.02** Laws, regulations, contracts, grant agreements, or policies frequently require the use of GAGAS. (See paragraph 1.04.) The following are among the laws, regulations, and guidelines that require the use of GAGAS:

**a.** The Inspector General Act of 1978, as amended, 5 U.S.C. App. requires that the statutorily appointed federal inspectors general comply with GAGAS for audits of federal establishments, organizations, programs, activities, and functions. The act further states that the inspectors general shall take appropriate steps to assure that any work performed by nonfederal auditors complies with GAGAS.

**b.** The Chief Financial Officers Act of 1990 (Public Law 101-576), as expanded by the Government Management Reform Act of 1994 (Public Law 103-356), requires that GAGAS be followed in audits of executive branch departments' and agencies' financial statements. The Accountability of Tax Dollars Act of 2002 (Public Law 107-289) extends this requirement to most executive agencies not subject to the Chief Financial Officers Act unless they are exempted for a given year by the Office of Management and Budget (OMB).

**c.** The Single Audit Act Amendments of 1996 (Public Law 104-156) require that GAGAS be followed in audits of state and local governments and nonprofit entities that receive federal awards.[104] OMB Circular No. A-133, *Audits of States, Local Governments, and Non-Profit Organizations*, which provides the governmentwide guidelines and policies on performing audits to comply with the Single Audit Act, also requires the use of GAGAS.

**A1.03** Other laws, regulations, or other authoritative sources may require the use of GAGAS. For example, auditors at the state and local levels of government may be required by state and local laws and regulations to follow GAGAS. Also, auditors may be required by the terms of an agreement or contract to follow GAGAS. Auditors may also be required to follow GAGAS by federal audit guidelines pertaining to program requirements, such as those issued for Housing and Urban Development programs and Student Financial Aid programs. Being alert to such other laws, regulations, or authoritative sources may assist auditors in performing their work in accordance with the required standards.

**A1.04** Even if not required to do so, auditors may find it useful to follow GAGAS in performing audits of federal, state, and local government programs as well as in performing audits of government awards administered by contractors, nonprofit entities, and other nongovernment entities. Many audit organizations not formally required to do so, both in the United States of America and in other countries, voluntarily follow GAGAS.

---

[104]Under the Single Audit Act, as amended, federal awards include federal financial assistance (grants, loans, loan guarantees, property, cooperative agreements, interest subsidies, insurance, food commodities, direct appropriations, or other assistance) and cost-reimbursement contracts.

## The Role of Those Charged with Governance in Accountability

**A1.05** During the course of GAGAS audits, auditors communicate with those charged with governance.

- For financial audits, see paragraphs 4.05 and 4.06.

- For attestation engagements, see paragraphs 6.06 through 6.08.

- For performance audits, see paragraphs 7.46 through 7.49.

**A1.06** Those charged with governance have the duty to oversee the strategic direction of the entity and obligations related to the accountability of the entity. This includes overseeing the financial reporting process, subject matter, or program under audit including related internal controls. In certain entities covered by GAGAS, those charged with governance also may be part of the entity's management. In some audit entities, multiple parties may be charged with governance, including oversight bodies, members or staff of legislative committees, boards of directors, audit committees, or parties contracting for the audit.

**A1.07** Because the governance structures of government entities and organizations can vary widely, it may not always be clearly evident who is charged with key governance functions. In these situations, auditors evaluate the organizational structure for directing and controlling operations to achieve the entity's objectives. This evaluation also includes how the government entity delegates authority and establishes accountability for its management personnel.

## Management's Role in Accountability

**A1.08** Government managers have fundamental responsibilities for carrying out government functions. (See paragraph 1.02.) Management of the audited entity is responsible for

**a.** using government resources legally, effectively, efficiently, economically, ethically, and equitably to achieve the purposes for which the resources were furnished or the program was established;[105]

**b.** complying with applicable laws and regulations (including identifying the requirements with which the entity and the official are responsible for compliance);

**c.** implementing systems designed to achieve compliance with applicable laws and regulations;

**d.** establishing and maintaining effective internal control to help ensure that appropriate goals and objectives are met; using resources efficiently, economically, effectively, and equitably, and safeguarding resources; following laws and regulations; and ensuring that management and financial information is reliable and properly reported;

**e.** providing appropriate reports to those who oversee their actions and to the public in order to demonstrate accountability for the resources and authority used to carry out government programs and the results of these programs;

**f.** addressing the findings and recommendations of auditors, and for establishing and maintaining a process to track the status of such findings and recommendations;

**g.** following sound procurement practices when contracting for audits and attestation engagements,

---

[105]This responsibility applies to all resources, both financial and physical, as well as informational resources, whether entrusted to public officials or others by their own constituencies or by other levels of government.

including ensuring procedures are in place for monitoring contract performance; and

**h.** taking timely and appropriate steps to remedy fraud, illegal acts, violations of provisions of contracts or grant agreements, or abuse that auditors report to it.

# Information to Accompany Chapter 3

**A3.01** Chapter 3 discusses the general standards applicable to financial audits, attestation engagements, and performance audits under GAGAS. Auditors may also provide professional services, other than audits and attestation engagements, which are sometimes referred to as nonaudit services or consulting services. GAGAS do not cover nonaudit services since such services are not audits or attestation engagements. If an audit organization decides to perform nonaudit services, their independence for performing audits or attestation engagements may be impacted. Nonaudit services which may impair or do impair auditor independence are discussed in chapter 3. (See paragraphs 3.20 through 3.30.) The following supplemental guidance is provided to assist auditors and audited entities in identifying nonaudit services that are often provided by audit organizations in government entities without impairing their independence with respect to entities for which they provide audits or attestation engagements.

# Nonaudit Services

**A3.02** Audit organizations in government entities frequently provide nonaudit services that differ from the traditional professional services provided by an accounting or consulting firm to or for the audited entity. These types of nonaudit services are often performed in response to a statutory requirement, at the discretion of the authority of the audit organization, or for a legislative oversight body or an independent external organization and do not impair auditor independence. (See paragraphs 3.20 through 3.30 for the requirements for evaluating whether nonaudit services impair auditor independence.)

**A3.03** Examples of these types of services include the following:

**a.** providing information or data to a requesting party without auditor evaluation or verification of the information or data;

**b.** developing standards, methodologies, audit guides, audit programs, or criteria for use throughout the government or for use in certain specified situations;

**c.** collaborating with other professional organizations to advance auditing of government entities and programs;

**d.** developing question and answer documents to promote understanding of technical issues or standards;

**e.** providing assistance and technical expertise to legislative bodies or independent external organizations and assisting legislative bodies by developing questions for use at a hearing;

**f.** providing training, speeches, and technical presentations;

**g.** developing surveys, collecting responses on behalf of others, and reporting results as "an independent third party";

**h.** providing oversight assistance in reviewing budget submissions;

**i.** contracting for audit services on behalf of an audited entity and overseeing the audit contract, as long as the overarching principles are not violated and the auditor under contract reports to the audit organization and not to management;

**j.** identifying good business practices for users in evaluating program or management system approaches, including financial and information management systems; and

**k.** providing audit, investigative, and oversight-related services that do not involve a GAGAS audit (but which could be performed as an audit, if the audit organization elects to do so), such as

**(1)** investigations of alleged fraud, violation of contract provisions or grant agreements, or abuse;

**(2)** review-level work such as sales tax reviews that are designed to review whether governmental entities receive from businesses, merchants, and vendors all of the sales taxes to which they are entitled;

**(3)** periodic audit recommendation follow-up engagements and reports;

**(4)** identifying best practices or leading practices for use in advancing the practices of government organizations;

**(5)** analyzing cross-cutting and emerging issues; and

**(6)** providing forward-looking analysis involving programs.

## System of Quality Control

**A3.04** Chapter 3 discusses the elements of an audit organization's system of quality control. The following supplemental guidance is provided to assist auditors and audit organizations in establishing policies and procedures in its system of quality control to address the following elements from paragraph 3.53: (1) audit and attestation engagement performance, documentation, and reporting and (2) monitoring of quality.

**a.** GAGAS standards for audit and attestation engagement performance, documentation, and reporting are in chapters 4 and 5 for financial audits, chapter 6 for attestation engagements, and chapters 7 and 8 for performance audits. Chapter 3 specifies that an audit organization's quality control system include policies and procedures designed to provide the audit organization with reasonable assurance that audits and attestation engagements are performed and reports are issued in accordance with professional standards and legal and regulatory requirements. (See paragraph 3.52) Examples of such policies and procedures include the following:

**(1)** communication provided to team members so that they sufficiently understand the objectives of their work and the applicable professional standards;

**(2)** audit and attestation engagement planning and supervision;

**(3)** appropriate documentation of the work performed;

**(4)** review of the work performed, the significant judgments made, and the resulting audit documentation and report;

**(5)** review of the independence and qualifications of any outside experts or contractors used, as well as a review of the scope and quality of their work;

**(6)** procedures for resolving difficult or contentious issues or disagreements among team members, including specialists;

(7) obtaining and addressing comments from the audited entity on draft reports; and

(8) reporting supported by the evidence obtained, and in accordance with applicable professional standards and legal and regulatory requirements.

**b.** Monitoring is an ongoing, periodic assessment of audit and attestation engagements designed to provide management of the audit organization with reasonable assurance that the policies and procedures related to the system of quality control are suitability designed and operating effectively in practice. (See paragraph 3.53f) The following guidance is provided to assist audit organizations with implementing and continuing its monitoring of quality:

(1) Who:  Monitoring is most effective when performed by persons who do not have responsibility for the specific activity being monitored (e.g., for specific engagements or specific centralized processes). The staff member or team of staff members assigned with responsibility for the monitoring process collectively need sufficient and appropriate competence and authority in the audit organization to assume that responsibility. Generally the staff member or the team of staff members performing the monitoring are apart from the normal audit supervision associated with individual audits.

(2) How much:  The extent of monitoring procedures varies based on the audit organization's circumstances to enable the audit organization to assess compliance with applicable professional standards and the audit organization's quality control policies and procedures. Examples of specific monitoring procedures include

(a) examination of selected administrative and personnel records pertaining to quality control;

(b) review of selected audit and attest documentation, and reports;

(c) discussions with the audit organization's personnel (as applicable and appropriate);

(d) periodic summarization of the findings from the monitoring procedures in writing, (at least annually), and consideration of the systematic causes of findings that indicate improvements are needed;

(e) determination of any corrective actions to be taken or improvements to be made with respect to the specific audits and attestation engagements reviewed or the audit organization's quality control policies and procedures;

(f) communication of the identified findings to appropriate audit organization management with subsequent follow-up; and

(g) consideration of findings by appropriate audit organization management personnel who also determine whether actions necessary, including necessary modifications to the quality control system, are performed on a timely basis.

(3) Review of selected administrative and personnel records: The review of selected administrative and personnel records pertaining to quality control may include tests of

(a) compliance with policies and procedures on independence;

(b) compliance with continuing professional development policies, including training;

(c) procedures related to recruitment and hiring of qualified personnel, including hiring of specialists or consultants when needed;

(d) procedures related to performance evaluation and advancement of personnel;

(e) procedures related to initiation, acceptance, and continuance of audit and attestation engagements;

(f) audit organization personnel's understanding of the quality control policies and procedures, and implementation of these policies and procedures; and

(g) audit organization's process for updating its policies and procedures.

**(4)** Follow-up on previous findings: Monitoring procedures include an evaluation of whether the audit organization has taken appropriate corrective action to address findings and recommendations from previous monitoring and peer reviews. Personnel involved in monitoring use this information as part of the assessment of risk associated with the design and implementation of the audit organization's quality control system and in determining the nature, timing, and extent of monitoring procedures.

**(5)** Written report: The audit organization communicates the results of the monitoring of its quality control systems in a written report that allows the audit organization to take prompt and appropriate action where necessary. Information included in this report includes:

(a) a description of the monitoring procedures performed;

(b) the conclusions drawn from the monitoring procedures; and

(c) where relevant, a description of the systemic, repetitive, or other significant deficiencies and of the actions taken to resolve those deficiencies.

**A3.05** As discussed in paragraph 3.61, an external audit organization should make its most recent peer review report publicly available. Examples of how to achieve this transparency requirement include posting the peer review report on an external Web site or to a publicly available file. To help the public understand the peer review reports, an audit organization may also include a description of the peer review process and how it applies to its organization. The following provides examples of additional information that audit organizations may include to help users understand the meaning of the peer review report.

**a.** Explanation of the peer review process.

**b.** Description of the audit organization's system of quality control.

**c.** Explanation of the relationship of the peer review results to the audited organization's work.

**d.** If the peer review report is modified, explanation of the reviewed audit organization's plan for improving quality controls and the status of the improvements.

## Information to Accompany Chapter 7

**A7.01** Chapter 7 discusses the field work standards for performance audits. An integral concept for performance auditing is the use of sufficient, appropriate evidence based on the audit objectives to support a sound basis for audit findings, conclusions, and recommendations. The following discussion is provided to assist auditors in identifying the various types of evidence and assessing the appropriateness of evidence in relation to the audit objectives.

## Types of Evidence

**A7.02** In terms of its form and how it is collected, evidence may be categorized as physical, documentary, or testimonial. Physical evidence is obtained by auditors' direct inspection or observation of people, property, or events. Such evidence may be documented in summary memos, photographs, videos, drawings, charts, maps, or physical samples. Documentary evidence is obtained in the form of already existing information such as letters, contracts, accounting records, invoices, spreadsheets, database extracts, electronically stored information, and management information on performance. Testimonial evidence is obtained through inquiries, interviews, focus groups, public forums, or questionnaires. Auditors frequently use analytical processes including computations, comparisons, separation of information into components, and rational arguments to analyze any evidence gathered to determine whether it is sufficient and appropriate. (See paragraphs 7.66 and 7.59 for definitions of sufficient and appropriate.) The strength and weakness of each form of evidence depends on the facts and circumstances associated with the evidence and professional judgment in the context of the audit objectives.

## Appropriateness of Evidence in Relation to the Audit Objectives

**A7.03** One of the primary factors influencing the assurance associated with a performance audit is the appropriateness of the evidence in relation to the audit objectives. For example:

**a.** The audit objectives might focus on verifying specific quantitative results presented by the audited entity. In these situations, the audit procedures would likely focus on obtaining evidence about the accuracy of the specific amounts in question. This work may include the use of statistical sampling.

**b.** The audit objectives might focus on the performance of a specific program or activity in the agency being audited. In these situations, the auditor may be provided with information compiled by the agency being audited in order to answer the audit objectives. The auditor may find it necessary to test the quality of the information, which includes both its validity and reliability.

**c.** The audit objectives might focus on information that is used for widely accepted purposes and obtained from sources generally recognized as appropriate. For example, economic statistics issued by government agencies for purposes such as adjusting for inflation, or other such information issued by authoritative organizations, may be the best information available. In such cases, it may not be practical or necessary for auditors to conduct procedures to verify the information. These decisions call for professional judgment based on the nature of the information, its common usage or acceptance, and how it is being used in the audit.

**d.** The audit objectives might focus on comparisons or benchmarking between various government functions or agencies. These types of audits are especially useful for analyzing the outcomes of various public policy decisions. In these cases, auditors may perform analyses, such as comparative statistics of different jurisdictions or changes in performance over time, where it would be impractical to verify the detailed data underlying the statistics. Clear disclosure as to what extent the comparative information or statistics were evaluated or corroborated will likely be necessary to place the evidence in proper context for report users.

**e.** The audit objectives might focus on trend information based on data provided by the audited entity. In this situation, auditors may assess the evidence by using overall analytical tests of underlying data, combined with a knowledge and understanding of the systems or processes used for compiling information.

**f.** The audit objectives might focus on the auditor identifying emerging and cross-cutting issues using information compiled or self-reported by agencies. In such cases, it may be helpful for the auditor to consider the overall appropriateness of the compiled information along with other information available about the program. Other sources of information, such as inspector general reports or other external audits, may provide the auditors with information regarding whether any unverified or self-reported information is consistent with or can be corroborated by these other external sources of information.

# Information to Accompany Chapter 8

**A8.01** Chapter 8 discusses the reporting standards for performance audits. The following discussion is provided to assist auditors in developing and writing their audit report for performance audits.

## Report Quality Elements

**A8.02** The auditor may use the report quality elements of timely, complete, accurate, objective, convincing, clear, and concise when developing and writing the auditor's report as the subject permits.

**a.** Accurate: An accurate report is supported by sufficient, appropriate evidence with key facts, figures, and findings being traceable to the audit evidence. Reports that are fact-based, with a clear statement of sources, methods, and assumptions so that report users can judge how much weight to give the evidence reported, assist in achieving accuracy. Disclosing data limitations and other disclosures also contribute to producing more accurate audit reports. Reports also are more accurate when the findings are presented in the broader context of the issue. One way to help audit organizations prepare accurate audit reports is to use a quality control process such as referencing. Referencing is a process in which an experienced auditor who is independent of the audit checks that statements of facts, figures, and dates are correctly reported, that the findings are adequately supported by the evidence in the audit documentation, and that the conclusions and recommendations flow logically from the evidence.

**b.** Objective: Objective means that the presentation of the report is balanced in content and tone. A report's credibility is significantly enhanced when it presents evidence in an unbiased manner and in the proper context. This means presenting the audit results impartially and fairly. The tone of reports may encourage decision makers to act on the auditors' findings and recommendations. This balanced tone can be achieved when reports present sufficient, appropriate evidence to support conclusions while refraining from using adjectives or adverbs that characterize evidence in a way that implies criticism or unsupported conclusions. The objectivity of audit reports is enhanced when the report explicitly states the source of the evidence and the assumptions used in the analysis. The report may recognize the positive aspects of the program reviewed if applicable to the audit objectives. Inclusion of positive program aspects may lead to improved performance by other government organizations that read the report. Audit reports are more objective when they demonstrate that the work has been performed by professional, unbiased, independent, and knowledgeable staff.

**c.** Complete: Being complete means that the report contains sufficient, appropriate evidence needed to satisfy the audit objectives and promote an understanding of the matters reported. It also means the report states evidence and findings without omission of significant relevant information related to the audit objectives. Providing report users with an understanding means providing perspective on the extent and significance of reported findings, such as the frequency of occurrence relative to the number of cases or transactions tested and the relationship of the findings to the entity's operations. Being complete also means clearly stating what was and was not done and explicitly describing data limitations, constraints imposed by restrictions on access to records, or other issues.

**d.** Convincing: Being convincing means that the audit results are responsive to the audit objectives, that the findings are presented persuasively, and that the conclusions and recommendations flow logically from the facts presented. The validity of the findings, the reasonableness of the conclusions, and the benefit of implementing the recommendations are more convincing when supported by sufficient, appropriate evidence. Reports designed in this way can help focus the attention of responsible officials on the matters that warrant attention and can provide an incentive for taking corrective action.

**e.** Clear: Clarity means the report is easy for the intended user to read and understand. Preparing the report in language as clear and simple as the subject permits assists auditors in achieving this goal. Use of straightforward, nontechnical language is helpful to simplify presentation. Defining technical terms, abbreviations, and acronyms that are used in the report is also helpful. Auditors may use a highlights page or summary within the report to capture the report user's attention and highlight the overall message. If a summary is used, it is helpful if it focuses on the specific answers to the questions in the audit objectives, summarizes the audit's most significant findings and the report's principal conclusions, and prepares users to anticipate the major recommendations. Logical organization of material, and accuracy and precision in stating facts and in drawing conclusions assist in the report's clarity and understanding. Effective use of titles and captions and topic sentences makes the report easier to read and understand. Visual aids (such as pictures, charts, graphs, and maps) may clarify and summarize complex material.

**f.** Concise: Being concise means that the report is not longer than necessary to convey and support the message. Extraneous detail detracts from a report, may even conceal the real message, and may confuse or distract the users. Although room exists for considerable judgment in determining the content of reports, those that are fact-based but concise are likely to achieve results.

**g.** Timely: To be of maximum use, providing relevant evidence in time to respond to officials of the audited entity, legislative officials, and other users' legitimate needs is the auditors' goal. Likewise, the evidence provided in the report is more helpful if it is current. Therefore, the timely issuance of the report is an important reporting goal for auditors. During the audit, the auditors may provide interim reports of significant matters to appropriate entity officials. Such communication alerts officials to matters needing immediate attention and allows them to take corrective action before the final report is completed.

# Comptroller General's Advisory Council on Government Auditing Standards

**Advisory Council Members**

Mr. Jack R. Miller, Chair
KMPG LLP (Retired)
(member 1997-1998; chair 2001-2008)

The Honorable Ernest A. Almonte
Office of the Auditor General
State of Rhode Island
(member 2001-2008)

Dr. Paul A. Copley
James Madison University
(member 2005-2008)

Mr. David Cotton
Cotton & Co. LLP
(member 2006-2009)

The Honorable Debra K. Davenport
Office of the Auditor General
State of Arizona
(member 2002-2005)

Ms. Kristine Devine
Deloitte & Touche, LLP
(member 2005-2008)

Dr. John H. Engstrom
Northern Illinois University
(member 2002-2005)

The Honorable Richard L. Fair
Office of the State Auditor
State of New Jersey
(member 2002-2005)

Dr. Ehsan Feroz
University of Minnesota Duluth
(member 2002-2009)

The Honorable Phyllis Fong
U.S. Department of Agriculture
(member 2004-2006)

Mr. Alex Fraser
Standard & Poor's
(member 2006-2009)

The Honorable Gregory H. Friedman
U.S. Department of Energy
(member 2002-2005)

Mr. Mark Funkhouser
Office of City Auditor (Retired)
Kansas City, Missouri
(member 2005-2008)

Dr. Michael H. Granof
University of Texas at Austin
(member 2005-2008)

Mr. Jerome Heer
Office of the County Auditor
Milwaukee, Wisconsin
(member 2004-2006)

Ms. Marion Higa
Office of State Auditor
State of Hawaii
(member 2006-2009)

The Honorable John P. Higgins, Jr.
U.S. Department of Education
(member 2005-2008)

Mr. Russell Hinton
Office of the State Auditor
State of Georgia
(member 2004-2006)

Mr. Richard A. Leach
United States Navy
(member 2005-2008)

Mr. Patrick L. McNamee
PricewaterhouseCoopers, LLP
(member 2005-2008)

Mr. Rakesh Mohan
Office of Performance Evaluations
Idaho State Legislature
(member 2004-2006)

The Honorable Samuel Mok
U.S. Department of Labor
(member 2006-2009)

Mr. Harold L. Monk
Davis Monk & Company, CPAs
(member 2002-2009)

Mr. William Monroe
Office of Auditor General
State of Florida
(member 2004-2006)

Mr. Stephen L. Morgan
Office of the City Auditor
Austin, Texas
(member 2001-2008)

Mr. Robert M. Reardon, Jr.
State Farm Insurance Companies
(member 2002-2005)

Mr. Brian A. Schebler
McGladrey & Pullen, LLP
(member 2005-2008)

Mr. Gerald Silva
Office of the City Auditor
San Jose, California
(member 2002-2009)

Mr. Barry R. Snyder
Federal Reserve Board (Retired)
(member 2001-2008)

Dr. Daniel Stufflebeam
Western Michigan University
(member 2002-2009)

The Honorable Nikki Tinsley
U.S. Environmental Protection Agency
(member 2002-2005)

Mr. George Willie
Bert Smith & Co.
(member 2004-2006)

## GAO Project Team

Jeffrey C. Steinhoff, Managing Director
Jeanette M. Franzel, Project Director
Robert F. Dacey, Chief Accountant
Abraham D. Akresh, Senior Level Expert for
    Auditing Standards
Marcia B. Buchanan, Specialist, Auditing Standards
Michael C. Hrapsky, Specialist, Auditing Standards
Heather I. Keister, Specialist, Auditing Standards
Gail Flister Vallieres, Specialist, Auditing Standards
Maxine L. Hattery,  Senior Communications Analyst
Margaret A. Mills, Senior Communications Analyst
Jennifer V. Allison, Council Administrator

# Index

**abuse** (see also attestation engagements, field work standards; attestation engagements, reporting standards; financial audits, field work standards; financial audits, reporting standards; performance audits, reporting standards; performance audits, field work standards) A.05–A.06

    examples of A.06

**accountability**

    governance, role of those charged with A1.05–A1.07

    government 1.01–1.02

    government managers and officials, responsibilities of 1.02, A1.08

**accurate, as report quality element** A8.02

**Advisory Council on Government Auditing Standards, members of** Appendix II

**agreed-upon procedures** (see attestation engagements, field work standards)

**AICPA standards**

    for attestation engagements 1.15a, 3.45, 6.01, 6.03–6.04, 6.06, 6.30

    for financial audits 1.15a, 3.44, 4.01, 4.03, 4.05, 4.19, 4.26–4.28, 5.01, 5.03, 5.15, 5.23, 5.26

    relationship to GAGAS 1.15a

**American Evaluation Association** 1.16

**American Institute of Certified Public Accountants** (see also AICPA standards) 1.15a

**American Psychological Association** 1.16

**appropriateness of evidence** 7.59–7.65, A7.03

**assurance** (see quality control and assurance; reasonable assurance)

**attestation engagements** (see also GAGAS)

    types of 1.23

    subject matter 1.24

    qualifications for auditors, additional 3.45

**attestation engagements, field work standards** 6.01–6.29

    abuse 6.13c–6.14

    agreed-upon-procedures–level engagement 1.23c, 6.13b

    AICPA standards 6.01, 6.03–6.06

    cause 6.18

    communication, auditor 6.06–6.08

    condition 6.17

    corrective actions 6.09, 6.18–6.19

    criteria 6.16

    documentation 6.07–6.08, 6.13a, 6.17, 6.20–6.26

    effect 6.19

    evidence 6.04b, 6.16, 6.18, 6.20–6.22

    examination-level engagements 1.23a, 6.10, 6.13a

criteria (*see* attestation engagements, field work standards; financial audits, field work standards; performance audits, field work standards)

data reliability (*see* information)

definitions (*see* terms)

documentation (*see also* attestation engagements, field work standards; financial audits, field work standards; financial audits, reporting standards; performance audits, field work standards)

    of continuing professional education 3.48–3.49

    of decisions using professional judgment 3.38

    GAGAS, departure from 1.07b

    GAGAS, significance of not complying with 1.12a

    of independence 3.08f, 3.15, 3.19, 3.30

    of quality control system 3.52–3.53

economy and efficiency audits (*see* performance audits)

effect (*see* attestation engagements, field work standards; financial audits, field work standards; performance audits, field work standards)

ethical principles 2.01–2.15

    conflicts, avoiding 2.10

    as framework 2.04

    and independence 2.03

    information, use of government 2.11–2.12

    integrity 2.03, 2.05b, 2.08–2.09

    objectivity 2.03, 2.05c, 2.10

    position, use of government 2.05d, 2.11, 2.14

    professional behavior 2.05e, 2.15

    public interest 2.03, 2.05a, 2.06–2.07

    resources, use of government 2.05d, 2.11, 2.13

    responsibility for, personal and organizational 2.03

    tone 2.01

    transparency 2.12

explanatory material 1.08–1.10

external quality control review (*see* peer review, external)

evidence (*see also* attestation engagements, field work standards; financial audits, field work standards; performance audits, field work standards; performance audits, reporting standards; information) 1.25–1.27, 7.55–7.71

    amount and type required, identifying 7.40

    appropriateness 7.56, 7.59–7.65, A7.01–A7.03

**fraud and illegal acts, indicators of risk of** (*see also* attestation engagements, field work standards; attestation engagements, reporting standards; financial audits, field work standards; financial audits, reporting standards; performance audits, field work standards; performance audits, reporting standards) A.07–A.08

**GAGAS** (*see also* attestation engagement, reporting standards; financial audits, field work standards; financial audits, reporting standards; performance audits, field work standards; performance audits, reporting standards) 1.01–1.34, A1.02-A1.04

application 1.03–1.04, A1.02–A1.04

for attestation engagements 1.03-1.04, 1.23–1.24

audits and attestation engagements, types of 1.17–1.20

compliance statements 1.11–1.13

departure from 1.07b, 1.12b–1.13, 4.21, 7.81

explanatory material 1.08–1.10

for financial audits 1.22

guidance, supplemental 1.21, A.01–A8.02

laws, regulations, and guidelines that require A1.02–A1.04

and nonaudit services 1.33–1.34

nongovernmental entities, applicability to 1.04

for performance audits 1.25–1.32

purpose 1.03

relationship to other standards 1.14–1.16

requirements, categories of 1.07

terminology, use of 1.05–1.10

**governance, role of those charged with** A1.05–A1.07

**government information, resources, and position, proper use of** 2.11–2.14

**guidance, supplemental** A.01–A8.02

abuse, examples of A.05–A.06

evidence in relation to audit objectives, appropriateness of A7.03

evidence, types of A7.01–A7.02

fraud risk indicators, examples of A.07–A.08

governance, role of those charged with A1.05–A1.07

government accountability, GAGAS in context of A1.01–A1.08

internal control deficiencies, examples of A.03–A.04

laws, regulations, and guidelines that require GAGAS A1.02–A1.04

laws, regulations, and provisions of contracts or grant agreements, significance to audit objectives A.09–A.11

management, role of A1.08

must and is required  1.07a

objectivity  2.10

outcomes  7.15g

outputs  7.15f

performance audit  1.25–1.28

presumptively mandatory requirement  1.07b

probable  footnotes 65, 85

professional behavior  2.15

professional judgment  3.32–3.34

professional skepticism  3.32

program  footnote 13

program operations  7.15e

proper use of government information, resources, and position  2.11–2.14

public interest  2.06–2.07

quality control, system of  3.51

reasonable assurance  4.01b, 7.03

reasonably possible  footnotes 65, 85

relevance  7.59a

reliability  7.59c

remote  footnotes 65, 85

requirement  1.05–1.07

unconditional requirement  1.07a

scope  7.09

should  1.07b

significance  footnote 28, 7.04

significant  footnote 89

significant deficiency  5.11a, 6.34a

specialist  footnote 21

subject matter  1.23–1.24

sufficiency  7.56, 7.66–7.67

sufficient, appropriate evidence  7.56

those charged with governance  footnotes 49, 80, 97; A1.06–A1.07

unmodified GAGAS compliance statement  1.12a

validity  7.59

**those charged with governance, in accountability communications**  A1.05–A1.07

attestation engagements  6.07–6.08

definition footnotes 49, 80, 97; A1.06–A1.07

financial audits 4.06–4.08

performance audits 7.46–7.49

**timely, as report quality element** A8.02g


**value-for-money audits** (*see* performance audits)

**views of responsible officials** (*see* attestation engagements, reporting standards; financial audits, reporting standards; performance audits, reporting standards)

**violations of contracts or grant agreements** (*see* attestation engagements, field work standards; attestation engagements, reporting standards; financial audits, field work standards; financial audits, reporting standards; performance audits, field work standards; performance audits, reporting standards)


**work of others, using** (*see also* attestation engagements, field work standards; financial audits, field work standards; performance audits, field work standards) 3.63